CHINA, TRADE AND POWER

CHINA, TRADE AND POWER

WHY THE WEST'S ECONOMIC ENGAGEMENT HAS FAILED

STEWART PATERSON

LONDON PUBLISHING PARTNERSHIP

Published by London Publishing Partnership
www.londonpublishingpartnership.co.uk

All Rights Reserved

ISBN: 978-1-907994-81-4 (hardback)

A catalogue record for this book is available from the
British Library

This book has been composed in Adobe Garamond Pro

Copy-edited and typeset by T&T Productions Ltd, London
www.tandtproductions.com

Cover design by James Shannon
www.jshannon.com

Printed and bound by TJ International Ltd, Padstow, Cornwall

CONTENTS

ACKNOWLEDGEMENTS

The aim of this book is to promote reasoned and informed debate on the economic relationship between the West and China. If this book helps bring to a wider audience an understanding of how important and all-pervasive this relationship has been and remains, it will have achieved its purpose. Through a better understanding of how we have arrived at the current trade challenges it is my hope that better policies will be implemented for the benefit of all.

I am extremely grateful to the Hinrich Foundation for their assistance in the production of this book. The Foundation is a non-partisan research organization committed to advancing the understanding of sustainable global trade. Through factual research and balanced analysis, the Foundation aims to encourage continued engagement in trade for mutually beneficial outcomes that support geopolitical stability.

INTRODUCTION: MAY YOU LIVE IN INTERESTING TIMES

It is not so long ago that a member of the Diplomatic Body in London, who had spent some years of his service in China, told me that there was a Chinese curse which took the form of saying, 'May you live in interesting times.' There is no doubt that the curse has fallen on us... We move from one crisis to another. We suffer one disturbance and shock after another.

— Sir Austen Chamberlain, 1936

NOT MANY PEOPLE COULD TELL you what happened on the 11th of December 2001, yet China's accession to the World Trade Organization (WTO) has transformed the lives of literally hundreds of millions of people both in China and beyond. In some ways, accession will define the economics and possibly the geopolitics of the twenty-first century. December the 11th is surely a contender for celebration, at least in China. However, from a Western point of view, the policy of economic engagement with China has failed. If the intention of the West was to mould China in its own image, the policy has been counterproductive. By enabling a rapid rise in living standards in China without political change, trade and investment have helped validate the policies of the Communist Party of China (CPC) and legitimize the regime. What were Western leaders thinking at the time? How did Western, market-orientated, property-owning, liberal democracy go from being in a position of complete global hegemony in the early 1990s to the current crisis of confidence? Can China's totalitarian model be contained?

This book tells the story of the most successful trading nation of the early twenty-first century, China, and its economic rise. It is the story of how the CPC has used trade to lift millions of Chinese out of abject poverty and how, in doing so, it has retained and cemented its monopoly of political power – producing undreamed of riches for the political elite. It is the most extraordinary economic success story of our time and has reshaped the geopolitics not just of Asia but of the world. As China has grown to dominate global manufacturing, its power and influence has grown as a producer, a customer and an investor. This economic power is being translated into political power and the West now has a global rival that is politically antithetical to liberal values. Perhaps more important than that, though, is the story of how the West has mishandled the consequences of economic engagement with China to the detriment of its own society. How, from a position of seeming dominance in the 1990s, does liberal democracy find itself in a crisis?

China traded with the world before joining the WTO, but the scale and depth of the economic engagement between China and the rest of the world changed beyond recognition in the years that followed her accession. Many of the most pressing economic, social and therefore political issues that we now face were either caused or accentuated by China's entry into the global trading system and the policy responses to it. Political and economic historians may well see it as marking 'peak liberalism' and the start of a move away from the unipolar world created by the fall of the Soviet empire. WTO accession was a diplomatic victory for China, which announced to the world that it was intent on playing its part in reforming the global order that had arisen after World War II. Her participation may end up destroying it.

Policymakers and opinion formers have consistently underestimated or downplayed the role that China's entry into the global economy has played in shaping the economic and social issues that the West, in particular, now faces. This may partly have been to avoid culpability or because the true extent of the consequences of interacting with China remains misunderstood. Avoidance of the issue, however, comes at price. Policy mistakes continue to be made, and these errors are compounding problems and threatening the social and economic order that has prevailed in the West for most of the post-war period. Democracy itself, in its modern form, is threatened. This is not a 'China-bashing' book and the blame, if indeed blame is the right word, does not necessarily lie with communist China. The Chinese leadership has, in some ways at least, served their population well as far as their international relations are concerned over the past twenty years. Accession to the WTO marked the culmination of fifteen years of diplomacy on the part of the CPC and although there have been victims in China, as a nation, communist China has been a winner from the process and its aftermath, at least in raw economic terms, and that was their aim.

The most immediate and direct impact of China's accession to the WTO was felt by the urban residents of China's eastern and southern coastal provinces. Their economic prospects had been improving steadily for twenty years as China gradually opened up to trade and experimented with various economic policies that deviated from the Maoist orthodoxy, but they were about to improve dramatically. In the first decade of the century, an additional 205 million people moved from the countryside to urban areas. Wages would rise twelvefold over the coming fifteen years. Cityscapes would be transformed. The physical appearance of society

changed beyond recognition. Developments that have taken decades or even generations in other societies would be crammed into
a few short years in China.

It was access to export markets that drove this transformative
wave of China's economic growth. WTO accession, with its guarantee of continued, unconditional access to these markets and
the commensurate foreign direct investment, turned what would
have been gradual progress into an apparently complete and rapid
economic transformation. To spread the wealth more evenly and
economic opportunity further afield, the proceeds from China's
export success were channelled into domestic infrastructure that
was built on a gargantuan scale. The pace of urbanization – 20 million new residents a year – demanded a rebuilding of the housing
stock. The size of China's construction industry became larger than
many national economies. As China's savings were funnelled into
the state-owned banking system, the biggest credit expansion in
history got underway. The destination of this lending was infrastructure and investment in an industrial complex that facilitated
the capture of market share in heavy industry and manufacturing
at an unprecedented speed.

Encouraged by the prevailing macroeconomic policy, consumers outside China, particularly in the West, lapped up the output
from China's new industrial complex, often borrowing to do so:
prices fell and volumes rose. White goods, toys, clothes and electronics products became available at prices that consumers could
not have imagined a few years earlier as China went from being
a relatively closed economy to having the largest share of global
exports since the level achieved by the United States in 1968. This
market share gain in world manufacturing exports, however, came
at a cost elsewhere, and not just in the developed world. In Mexico,
which had been America's low-cost manufacturing centre, wages
began to stagnate. Even now, average wages are at the same level
as they were in US dollar terms in 1990. At the outset of NAFTA,

one could be forgiven for believing that Mexico's economy would converge with that of the United States in much the same way as East Germany's would with West Germany, yet it has not happened. In many ways, Mexico now has some of the hallmarks of a failing state.

There were winners too. The fortunes of Australia's mining industry contrasted dramatically with those of Mexico's manufacturers, at least temporarily. Here, the state capitalism of China, with its propensity to invest in ever greater capacity irrespective of the economic returns, produced a boom of unprecedented size. China's investment in steel capacity, power generation and a range of other mineral-intensive industries produced an unprecedented growth in demand for mining products from Australia. Parts of Canada and Brazil had a similar experience and the Gulf states were physically transformed on the back of revenue from high oil prices as China's state-owned oil companies failed to deliver the growth in production that was required by the rapidly urbanizing and industrializing Chinese economy. China's rise has been a boon for those countries blessed with the commodities China has needed.

The ramifications of allowing this kind of free trade were bound to be severe. On the one hand, we had a nation of 1.2 billion people (as it was then, 1.4 billion now) with an average income of less than $1,000 a year, and on the other we have the developed-world economies of America, Japan and parts of Europe with labour costs twenty times higher and a combined population of around 900 million. In the developed world, these ramifications started to manifest themselves in falling living standards for those who were competing for jobs with the new trading partner. Manufacturing jobs vanished from the West. Manufacturing employment in the US shrank by 5 million in the first decade of the millennium while China added 15 million manufacturing jobs. Economic performance in the developed world began to stagnate in the first decade of the twenty-first century and what growth there was came at an increasing cost: inequality in outcomes increased, investment fell, productivity growth declined and debt levels rose. Economic prospects seemed to become increasingly binary. The flip side of the changing skylines of China and the Middle East was the rising unemployment and the hollowing out of industrial communities in Europe and the US to create crime-ridden, welfare-dependent, post-industrial wastelands.

The efficacy of monetary policy – its ability to stimulate job growth – appeared to be waning in a globalized world. Ever more debt was required to sustain aggregate employment in the face of low-cost Chinese labour. The deflationary pressure that cheap exports from China exerted on developed economies, coupled with a central bank policy of inflation targeting, resulted in unusually easy monetary policy in much of the world. The old, tried-and-tested response to an economic slowdown of lowering interest rates no longer seemed to work with the same vigour as in the past, and China's currency intervention prevented the natural adjustment in exchange rates from taking place. Debts mounted up both in China and outside. Asset bubbles formed as nominal rates remained low, and the consequent increased financial leverage came with risks that have since become all too apparent. America's debt-fuelled housing bubble and collapse followed directly from China's WTO entry. The subsequent deflationary pressure, the monetary response to try to prevent deflation and the malfeasance that accompanied this monetary free-for-all have discredited capitalism in the eyes of large segments of the Western population.

The beneficiaries of asset price inflation in the West owe a lot to China and its export success following accession to the WTO, although few probably recognize that fact. If you were lucky enough to own assets, you have done well; if you used leverage to do so, you have done even better. The price rises of financial assets and real estate have far outpaced the rise in the income streams that support those valuations. For those who were too young to climb aboard the train, home ownership for many is a distant dream and purchasing an old-age income for retirement with interest rates at or near zero is prohibitively expensive. The generational divide caused by asset price inflation is just one of the societal schisms that has arisen as a result of the reaction of Western central banks to deflationary pressure.

If the economic impact has been divisive, with winners and losers both inside and outside China, the political impact has been disappointing for those who championed Chinese membership of the WTO in the belief that the institution would bring pluralism to China. Prosperity, they argued, would change Chinese politics. The new middle class would demand political reform and representation. Totalitarianism could not survive exposure to world trade, a rules-based system and a dispute-resolution mechanism. Democratization was to be the inevitable result of rising living standards and exposure to Western institutions. Many Chinese conservatives shared this view and were wary of and opposed membership as a result. For the very same reasons, some Chinese dissidents supported it.

Seventeen years later, the CPC appears to be as in control as ever. If there was a risk to the CPC it was that a failure to deliver on material living standards would lead to its overthrow. If trade helped China transform its economy, then, for the time being at least, it appears it helped the CPC consolidate their grip on power too. Of course, rapid economic development has also produced social schisms in China. Income inequality rivals that in America and a disproportionate share of the economic spoils have accrued to leading members of the CPC, but so far the security apparatus has proved itself more than capable of containing any protest. China remains a society ruled by law rather than enjoying the rule of law, where the Party and the State are to all intents and purposes the same thing.

It is not the old political order in China that has been most threatened, as was expected by some, by her new trading relationship with the rest of the world but the political order of the West. While Xi Jinping consolidates the power of the Communist Party and basks in the glory of economic advancement, Western society appears to be undergoing a crisis of confidence. It is rare to hear politicians espouse market-orientated solutions to the problems of globalization. In the face of China's mercantilist policies, a laissez-faire approach was perhaps bound to produce too many unfair outcomes for free-market economics to sustain its moral high ground.

Many of the social programmes that formed the backbone of the social contract between the liberal democratic state and its population have never been stress tested against the demographics that the West now faces, nor have its governments had to contend with a prolonged period of low nominal gross domestic product (GDP) growth and stagnant incomes brought about by falling productivity growth and low inflation. This is important because the Western democratic model has, for at least seventy years, required government expenditure to exceed revenue, with the real value of the resulting debt being inflated away. Democratic politics, in its modern form, has become little more than an auction for the support of vested interest groups by promising state-funded assistance in the provision of life's necessities and indeed sometimes luxuries too. The problem with robbing Peter to pay Paul (or more precisely to buy his vote) is that in a democracy you need more Pauls than Peters and so governments tend to run deficits. Without inflation and growth, deficits and debt become unsustainable. The ensuing austerity has had a further fragmenting impact on society.

Publicly funded or subsidized health provision and pensions are the two main and obvious examples of where the social contract in the West is under pressure. Both require ever rising nominal GDP to at least provide the illusion of sustainability, but the combination of poor demographics (a shrinking labour force) and deflationary pressure makes high nominal GDP growth hard to achieve. Productivity growth, the third leg to the stool, has been elusive partly due to the fact that so much of the world's investment has been taking place in China and cheap labour was an alternative to innovation. Low inflation or, even worse, deflation puts the sustainability of government borrowing at risk. Inflation erodes the real value of a government's debt – its past borrowings or deficits – thus making it easier to service and pay back. Without inflation, as we have recently seen in Greece and to a lesser extent in Spain and Portugal, savers quickly question the sustainability of deficit financing. China did not force European countries to abandon their monetary independence and unite under the euro, but their exportation of deflation has exposed the potential folly of the project much faster than would otherwise have been the case. Public confidence in elected officials is at an all-time low and this is reflected in desperately low voter turnout in support of mainstream political parties. Ironically, Western populations expect more from government now than any previous generation, yet have no faith in their ability to deliver. And to think it was Western governments – proponents of China's accession to the WTO – who hoped engagement with the West would wean the Chinese population off government dependency.

Perhaps the most damning interpretation of the consequences of China's accession to the WTO and the policy of unconditional economic engagement with China is that accession not only acted as an endorsement of a totalitarian regime, but by providing a platform for economic success, it perpetuated it. By allowing permanent access to export markets, it fuelled an economic transformation that has inadvertently cemented the Communist Party in power. The much-hoped-for rule of law, advancement of human rights and move towards a pluralistic, free and open society has failed to materialize in China. To boot, economic prowess has been turned into increasing military power. Liberal democracies now face a geopolitical rival in the ascendancy in Asia and beyond, which has the potential to impose a large cost on the West for the maintenance of its freedoms. Inevitably, the convergence of China's living standards towards the global average will require natural resources that China does not possess, and securing them could lead China into conflict with other countries. By helping to facilitate economic maturity without political plurality, economic engagement has created a whole new area of potential conflict. Worse still for democrats, China's international prestige is now such that her totalitarian model is seen by some as a credible alternative to Western liberalism. Conversely, post-war Western institutions have been eroded by engagement with China. Western society has been further fragmented along geographical and generational lines. Economic liberalism has lost its moral foundation, in part because economic outcomes are not perceived to be the result of fair competition. The weaknesses of our democratic model are being laid bare and consequently the ideal itself is being challenged. In the hubris that followed the collapse of the Soviet Union, liberal democracies may well have overestimated their own strength.

Perhaps, it could be argued, opening the economies of the developed world to 1.2 billion people with a per capita income one-thirtieth of that in the West, operating a very different legal, political and social framework, was always going to have profound ramifications. If the West has now embarked on a change of direction regarding its policy towards China, to become less indulgent and more competitive – then it is surely of the utmost importance that we understand the true and full extent of how a policy of engagement has moulded Western society in recent years. Only then might the right policy steps be taken, and the right organizations created to preserve and spread affluence while protecting Western freedoms.

Chapter 1

Unconditional Economic Engagement: Motives for WTO Membership

If we treated China as an enemy, we were guaranteeing an enemy in the future. If we treated China as a friend, we could not guarantee friendship, but we kept open the possibility of more benign futures.

——Joseph Nye, American political scientist

O N THE 11TH OF DECEMBER 2001 China acceded to the World Trade Organization (WTO) after fifteen years of negotiations. The process had lasted so long that the organization China had initially applied to join, the General Agreement on Tariffs and Trade (GATT), had ceased to exist and been replaced by the WTO in 1994. Few people have heard of Long Yongtu, but he was primarily responsible for the negotiations on China's behalf throughout much of the process that culminated in membership of the world trade body – an event that ultimately helped change China's economic performance beyond recognition and, as Napoleon had predicted, 'shook the world'. Such was the concern regarding China's membership that no less than thirty-seven members of the WTO asked for bilateral agreements prior to accession.

China's WTO accession did not mark the beginning of economic engagement with China, but it did move trade and investment onto a more permanent and elevated plane by bringing the process inside the multilateral framework.

At one level it is easy to understand why China's Communist Party leadership were keen to join the WTO and why, as the 1990s progressed, it became a higher priority for them. The massacre in Tiananmen Square in 1989 and the international backlash against it highlighted the vulnerability of China's nascent export sector to political events at home and their impact on overseas opinion. Furthermore, the collapse of the Soviet Union demonstrated the potential political price of economic failure. While economic progress seemed to come relatively easily to some Asian countries embracing market-orientated economic policies, the demise of the Soviet empire laid bare the potential failings of a centrally planned system. In the Soviet case, these shortcomings were of a scale that surprised even the most sceptical of outside observers. China was keen to learn the lessons of Russian failure. Foremost among these was that isolation from the technological progress that Western societies were making almost guaranteed subordination in the world order. The country desperately needed know-how and skills, and this was only likely to come from abroad if it was tied into a rules-based trade system, which meant WTO membership. Not being a member was holding back technology transfer and foreign direct investment (FDI), which, in turn, was preventing China from taking, as they saw it, its rightful place in the world as a leading power. Non-membership also threatened the CPC's ability to deliver better living standards to the population.

Secondly, as one of the five permanent members of the UN Security Council, there was a clear sense that China was missing out on an important seat at the table that oversaw global trade. By 2001 there were 140 members of the WTO, and China was conspicuous by her absence. She was, after all, by virtue of her vast population if nothing else, the seventh largest trading nation. The sense that China was not being given the recognition that she deserved in the international arena was acutely felt among many Chinese. As an ancient civilization and with the largest population of any country on earth at the time, China felt she should be accorded the trappings of a global power and that meant admission to all the institutions that claimed to be part of the multilateral framework of government. With the collapse of the Soviet Union and the inclusion of former members of the Warsaw Pact in the WTO, China's exclusion was looking increasingly anomalous in a more inclusive world order. The WTO was not, after all, the preserve of democracies. Over the longer term, a clear strategic aim of the Chinese was to gradually reshape the multilateral order to work in their interests and not exclusively, as they saw it, in those of the West. Long journeys start with a single step and membership of the WTO was that step.

Perhaps most pressing, though, was the need for more export-orientated growth. While the Chinese economy had been growing spectacularly since Deng Xiaoping kick-started economic reform in the late 1970s, China was still an economic non-entity in 1985 when it started the accession process. The base was so low that, despite rapid progress, China was still a modest economic power in the run-up to WTO accession. Furthermore, the growth rate was slowing. The Asian crisis of 1997/98 had blown the theory of Asian exceptionalism out of the water. The so-called Asian miracle looked more like a mirage. Asia was subject to the same laws of economics as anywhere else. There had been a very real drag on the performance of the Chinese economy from the impact of the Asian crisis but, more importantly, the reform process in China was producing significant economic and social problems that were homemade. Reform of state-owned enterprises (SOEs) had added perhaps 30 million to the ranks of the unemployed. Official unemployment statistics are nonsense in China, but academic estimates put the rate of urban unemployment in the late 1990s at 12–15%.[1] GDP growth that had been in the high teens in the early 1990s had started to slow in the middle of the decade and by China's own standards the economy was starting to stagnate at a growth rate of 5–7% based on official numbers that were probably overstating reality. By many estimates this was deemed the bare minimum to absorb urban population growth and prevent serious social disorder. The whole market-orientated reform programme was being questioned by many in China. It was far from a foregone conclusion that China would continue down the road of economic liberalization. Reform can mean different things to different people, and very few Chinese policymakers wanted a carbon copy of Western economic norms in China. Advocates of a 'socialist-market economy with Chinese characteristics' had everything still to prove. Accession to the WTO, and with it a boost to exports, could provide the breathing space to tackle some of the divisive issues that economic reform had thrown up.

From the perspective of the CPC, WTO accession was not without its risks. The social contract that had evolved between the Party and the population was now results-based and not ideological. The Party's *raison d'être* was to deliver higher living standards, or at least that is how a good proportion of the population saw it. In the absence of a democratic mandate, legitimacy came through success. Free trade, though, would expose China's backward SOEs to international competition. Many were already hopelessly loss making and more competition could kill them off altogether. What China needed was access to overseas markets, technology transfer and foreign investment but also a tightly controlled and gradual raising of the competitive temperature at home, so its own economic institutions could adapt to the more competitive environment without succumbing to it. To this end China sought to join the WTO as a 'developing country' to slow the pace of market exposure to foreign competition.

A second major risk for the CPC was the sensitivity of large areas of the economy that overlapped with their political aims and that were therefore crucial to the maintenance of the Party's influence. These included the state-owned banking system that allocated capital, the media that propagated the CPC agenda, and the telecommunications industry that enabled monitoring and control of information. These were areas where Western economies had a comparative advantage and superior know-how, and so the Party was determined to keep these areas strictly off-limits.

Finally, there was the issue of national sovereignty. If improving the economic lot of the population was one pillar of CPC legitimacy, protecting and enhancing the territorial integrity of China and its sovereignty was another. The legacy of the unequal treaties of the nineteenth century remain a part of China's national psychology. To the extent that membership of multilateral organizations could be perceived as handing foreigners a say in the running of China's affairs, it presented a threat to the power of the Party. China, after all, likes to portray itself as 'the most humiliated country' of the last century, a label used to justify jingoism when required or expedient. Those advocating and negotiating membership of the WTO were often accused of treasonous behaviour by the more nationalistic in China. Therefore, it was imperative that the economic benefits were quickly seen, and that foreign interference was kept to a minimum and shown to be ineffective.

There were other political risks too. It would be wrong to think that anything other than a very small percentage of the party were committed to democratization. Those that were had suffered a big setback as a result of the Tiananmen Square massacre. A slightly larger share might have thought some political change inevitable, but by and large there was no sense that economic reform need be a precursor to the loss of the CPC's monopoly of political power. The risk was, however, that economic liberalization and legal change, brought about by WTO membership, would lead to greater, even uncontrollable, demands for political change. This had to be weighed against the risk of what would happen if, by not opening up the economy more, economic performance disappointed and the CPC was seen to be failing. Here the Soviet example had been reinforced by events in Indonesia, where economic failure had swept the Suharto regime from power in 1998.

Jiang Zemin had become General Secretary of the Central Committee of the Communist Party in 1989, replacing Zhao Ziyang. Among senior communist officials, Zhao was probably the most ideologically committed to both economic and political reform but he was purged in 1989 for his support of the pro-democracy students. The student protests, which ended in the massacre, had initially begun as a commemoration of the death of Hu Yaobang, who along with Zhao had led the liberalizing element within the CPC through the 1980s. With both Zhao and Hu out of the way, the more conservative, or at least centrist, elements of the party were in the ascendency. Jiang became president of China in 1993 on the retirement of Yang Shangkun, and came to represent the 'core' of the third generation of post-revolutionary Chinese leadership. While many in the West saw the protests in Tiananmen Square as evidence that, with the right encouragement and incentives, political reform would come to China, in many ways it could be argued that the massacre of the 4th of June put an end to any such hopes. With genuine reformers out of contention for high office, and with Deng Xiaoping's backing – he was to die in 1993 – Jiang was able to consolidate power. True, Zhu Rongji, Jiang's chosen premier to replace the both economically and politically conservative Li Peng, certainly believed that market forces could be harnessed to improve economic efficiency and help cement the Communist Party's grip on power, but he was a committed economic reformer, not a democrat. He pushed economic reform vigorously, realizing that the CPC's legitimacy depended on improving economic outcomes. To Zhu and others, political reform consisted of clamping down on corruption and improving administration. There was very little in the make-up of the Chinese leadership, in the run-up to WTO accession, that should have encouraged Western policy-makers to believe that political reform, in the sense of a challenge to the CPC's monopoly of power, was likely to feature on the policy agenda other than perhaps an entrenched sense of the superiority of the democratic model and wishful thinking.

> China is a one-party state that does not tolerate opposition. It does deny citizens fundamental rights of free speech and religious expression. It does defend its interests in the world, and sometimes in ways that are dramatically at odds from our own. But the question is not whether we approve or disapprove of China's practices. The question is, what's the smartest thing to do to improve these practices?[2]

To President Clinton, and many other Western proponents of Chinese membership of the WTO, the answer to the question was obvious: expose China to Western economics, integrate them into the global order and the rest would follow. No totalitarian regime would be able to survive the onslaught of fast food (KFC was a big and early investor in China) and consumerism. Multinational companies and their products were the new weaponry in the war against tyranny. Controlling the internet, he said, was 'like trying to nail Jello to the wall.' Exposure to Western lifestyles, technology and culture would loosen and eventually prize open the communist grip on the population. It had after all been, in part, the craving of Eastern Europe's population for a materially better standard of living and the failure of the command economies to deliver it that had led to the collapse of the Berlin Wall. Consumer sovereignty and democracy, it was hoped, went hand in hand. This thought had occurred to some Chinese dissidents too. 'Before the sky was black: now there is a light,' said Ran Wanding, a Chinese human rights activist often quoted by Clinton, expressing his hope that a freer China would emerge from a more liberal open economy. Ran's hope was shared by many in China: that exposure to trade, to a rules-based economic system, Western ideas and culture would result in rising affluence and, with it, political change in China. To them free trade required the rule of law and improved the human condition, and the outside world would insist on it. Plenty of others disagreed.

Clinton went further:

> By lowering the barriers that protect state-owned industries, China is speeding a process that is removing government from vast areas of people's lives. In the past, virtually every Chinese citizen woke up in an apartment or a house owned by the government, went to work in a factory or a farm run by the government, and read newspapers published by the government. State-run workplaces also operated the schools where they sent their children, the clinics where they received health care, the stores where they bought food. That system was a big source of the Communist Party's power.[3]

As the private sector stepped up to provide employment and opportunity for the people, the invisible hand would replace the iron fist of the state. The Party would be rolled back out of people's lives and eventually become an irrelevance to an aspirant, modern, urban and prosperous China.

Human rights organizations were perhaps more cautious, with some very much opposed to engagement with China. But most had realistically low expectations from letting China into the WTO. As Mike Jendrzejczky, the much-respected Washington director of Human Rights Watch for Asia, put it:

> As a WTO member, China will commit itself to respecting global trading rules. This is a step towards China's

integration into the international system regulating not only trade relations but also governments' treatment of their own citizens. Restructuring China's economy to fit WTO standards will give a boost to those within China arguing that it must further open up both politically and economically if it is to be a respected member of the international community. But WTO membership will not itself lead to political changes.[4]

Madeleine Albright, the Secretary of State, said:

China's entry into the WTO is not a human rights issue – but it can only help the human rights and the political situation in China.[5]

The problem was that while the WTO accession process was ongoing, the US and others could use trade to gain some leverage over Chinese domestic policy, but once membership was secured that leverage was vastly if not entirely reduced.

That reduction in bilateral negotiating power was a function of the nature of the institution China was trying to join. So why did so many people profess such faith that membership of this organization would change a totalitarian regime? The World Trade Organization grew out of the failed attempt to form an international trade body to stand beside the World Bank and the International Monetary Fund as UN-sponsored economic institutions to oversee the new world economic order following World War II. To restart global trade after the war, the US and her allies signed the General Agreement on Tariffs and Trade in 1948. The hope was that this agreement would form the basis for the formation of the International Trade Organization (ITO). Ironically, China was a signatory to the original GATT and it was the failure of the US to sign up to the ITO, due to concerns about its impingement on national sovereignty, that led to the scrapping of the ITO and the continuation of GATT.

China's membership of GATT lapsed in the aftermath of China's civil war that followed victory over Japan and its isolation from the West pending recognition of the People's Republic of China as a legitimate regime. China formally applied to rejoin GATT in 1985 but membership, as a communist country, and one of her scale, was always going to be problematic politically and economically. Unlike GATT, the WTO had formal dispute-resolution mechanisms and gave member states the ability to punish those who broke the rules they had signed up to. As such it marked a big step forward in the process of building a legally enforceable framework for regulating international trade. Membership of the WTO was therefore a prerequisite for having any influence over the development of international trade policy and regulation. The WTO provided not only the forum for trade negotiation but also administered existing multilateral agreements with a purview extending beyond trade in goods to include services and the trade-related aspects of intellectual property rights.

Trade in the US and elsewhere has always been highly political: trade disputes with Great Britain were after all a major cause for the creation of the nation. Since the 1970s American presidents had granted waivers to China from the provisions of the Jackson–Vanik amendment to the 1974 Trade Act. This amendment, aimed largely at the Soviet Union and its satellite states, denies Most Favoured Nation (MFN) status to non-market countries that prohibit or restrict emigration. As Clinton pointed out, trade involves much more than the mere exchange of goods. Under the provisions of the Jackson–Vanik amendment, each year the President of the United States would have to grant a waiver which would ensure that, for the next twelve months, China could trade normally with the US. This waiver, however, could be overridden by Congress, so there was an annual congressional debate on the subject and the arguments for and against trade with China were held up for scrutiny. This became a forum for an audit of China's human rights abuses and progress on economic reform and hence of the suitability of China as a trading partner. Given the permanent nature of WTO arrangements and their potential conflict with the Jackson–Vanik amendment, Chinese membership of the WTO would first require that the US grant Permanent Normal Trade Relations (PNTR) to China. By granting PNTR, however, the annual debate on China's status would no longer be required and the US, through the WTO, would be tied into trade with China. Much of the leverage that the US had over China would disappear at a stroke.

Advocates of granting PNTR made some constructive arguments. They argued that a more open trading relationship with China would accelerate political reform and hence the advancement of human rights. Furthermore, exposure to, and forced compliance with, a rules-based international trade system would speed up economic reform and make domestic economic regulation more transparent. Together, these two factors would help make China more like the West. Additionally, they argued that since US markets were already open to Chinese goods through the annual granting of MFN status, PNTR followed by WTO membership would be a 'one-way street' opening Chinese markets to US companies. The WTO would force China to stop obstructing the existing theoretical access to markets in China that foreign companies enjoyed and make them a reality. Tariffs would be cut and, under the WTO, access to the all-important market in services would be to the benefit of US companies. WTO rules would guarantee intellectual property rights too so high-tech companies would have nothing to fear from Chinese trade and investment. As the Cato Institute put it:

> The economic benefits of granting PNTR to the United States are clear. As the U.S. market is already largely open

to Chinese imports, it is primarily U.S. exporters who will benefit. Granting PNTR to China will enable U.S. companies to take full advantage of the sweeping market access provisions that China has agreed to adopt in order to comply with WTO rules and obligations.[6]

With this new transparency and openness, competition in the Chinese economy was likely to intensify. Since state companies subjected to competition would inevitably lose market share once their protection was removed, so the argument ran, whole swathes of the Chinese economy would become the domain of the private sector and the state monopolies would be rolled back. The rise of the private sector was already an established trend in China, but WTO membership would help lock in the progress made so far and prevent any backsliding towards old-style communism. Lastly, because of greater market access for US companies in China, very specifically, the trade deficit with China, which had been a source of contention and concern and potential economic and financial risk, would disappear or at least meaningfully diminish. Furthermore, any further loss of employment because of manufacturing moving offshore would be more than compensated for by the creation of high-value jobs related to US access to Chinese markets for corporate services, finance and technology. Perhaps this view was most forcefully and succinctly put by Doug Bandow of the Cato Institute when he wrote:

> The silliest argument against PNTR is that Chinese imports would overwhelm U.S. industry. In fact, American workers are far more productive than their Chinese counterparts. Moreover, Beijing's manufacturing exports to the United States remain small about half the level of those from Mexico. PNTR would create far more export opportunities for American than Chinese concerns.[7]

In addition to these positive and constructive arguments for granting PNTR there were some more defensive and nuanced ones. If the US did not proceed, what message would this send to China? President Clinton argued:

> We must continue to defend our interests and our ideals with candor and consistency. But we can't do that by isolating China from the very forces most likely to change it. Doing so would be a gift to the hard-liners in China's government.

The 'anti-democrats and hardliners' would capitalize on this obfuscation and use it as evidence that the US was hell-bent on denying China its natural place in the world. Furthermore:

> Voting against PNTR won't free a single prisoner or create a single job in America or reassure a single American ally in Asia. It will simply empower the most rigid anti-democratic elements in the Chinese government.[8]

Further still, proponents of PNTR played on the fear that the US would be left behind in the race to sell to 1.2 billion eager consumers. Would not the Europeans and Japanese clean up in China as US companies would be disadvantaged by the apparent opposition and antagonism of Congress to the Chinese regime? Why deliberately put US companies at the back of the queue? This was a repeat of the arguments used by the more pragmatic or Sinophile (depending on your standpoint) elements of the UK's Foreign Office in the early 1980s during negotiations pertaining to the handover of Hong Kong to China. There was a big difference, however. Clinton was making the argument about corporates domiciled in the largest and most hegemonic economy the world has ever seen. Furthermore, it would not have been beyond the skill of US diplomats to corral both Japan and Europe (the

EU represents European Sovereign Nations in the WTO) into a co-conspiracy to deny China WTO accession should they have wished to do so.

In Europe, the political spectrum was divided along similar lines to those in the US. One big difference was that national governments had little to do with the negotiations as it was the EU that was responsible for the bilateral agreement with China. This meant that political debate on the issue was more limited. A government of any political colour was well placed to deflect criticism from its local populace by pointing to the pooled nature of national sovereignty within the EU structure. So while both George Bush and Bill Clinton, both directly elected, were in favour of China joining the WTO (albeit Clinton was initially keen to attach membership to progress on human rights) and Congress had a very public and open debate on the pros and cons of Chinese accession, it was career civil servant Pascal Lamy, the unelected European Commissioner for Trade (1999–2004), who concluded the negotiations on behalf of the EU (throughout most of the process, the Trade Commissioner responsible for heading the EU's negotiating effort had been Leon Brittan).

The relative de-politicization of trade negotiations in Europe opened the door for a far more Realpolitik approach. Furthermore, the various EU institutions could often espouse very different views about Chinese accession, and not necessarily because of a diversity of opinions among member states. The democratically elected, and therefore relatively accountable, European parliament was far more concerned with human rights and the moral dimension to engagement with China than the European Commission, for example. The Council of Ministers, composed of the heads of the various national governments, was likewise more responsive to public opinion than the Commission.

From the outset, the European Commission was an aggressive champion of China's accession to the WTO and broad engagement with China. German machine-tool companies, as it turned out, were to do well from supplying capital goods to China as it built up its manufacturing industry. The European Commission of the late 1990s was far more interventionist in an economic sense than the US government. Airbus, in its rivalry with Boeing, was a major factor in shaping Commission attitudes towards economic engagement with China. China bought USD1.2 billion of Airbus planes in 1996 to punish the US for trying to attach political conditions to trade. In this case it was to do with sanctions in retaliation for China's failure to crack down on the pirating of CDs and DVDs. Ironically, it was Bertelsmann of Germany and Sony Music's respective US subsidiaries that had lobbied the Clinton administration for support, but Japan and the EU had failed to back the US, making the threat of sanctions unilateral and therefore ineffective.[9]

To what extent the EU's accommodation of China altered the balance of power in terms of Sino–US negotiations is debatable. The US's attempt to tie Chinese accession to the WTO closely to specific progress on human and political rights failed. With hindsight, given the very unequal impact of China's accession, the Commission's relative acquiescence to China, which at times appeared to border on the sycophantic, could be seen as damaging to liberal Western interests. That was certainly Winston Lord's view when he accused the Japanese and Europeans of 'holding our coat tails while gobbling up our contracts'.[10] Since accession, the EU has been as vocal as the US in highlighting China's unfair trade practices and it is far from clear that the EU gained any lasting advantage over the US in its engagement with China because of its approach. The EU's importance to China was limited in terms of international relations and was to some extent confined to being a foil for US negotiating obduracy.

If the European Commission was the driving political force behind European acquiescence to China's desire for accession, in the US it was the corporate lobby. Big business had two objectives: to exploit cheap Chinese labour to lower costs and to gain market access to the Chinese population of 1.2 billion – potentially the largest market in the world. If the West saw irony in the CPC turning to a form of capitalism to deliver economic results, surely the CPC saw the irony in using the profit motive to manipulate the political behaviour of corporate America and have them do their bidding for them. In January 1993, William Jefferson Clinton had become the 42nd President of the United States, with the expressed intention of linking America's future economic engagement with China to progress on political and human rights. Throughout 1993 and the early part of 1994 China launched a charm offensive on corporate America. By dangling the carrot of profit in front of America's largest corporations, the Chinese were able to assemble a formidable lobby to campaign not only for the extension of China's MFN status but ultimately to put normal trade relations on a permanent footing and gain accession to the WTO. Such was the success of China's efforts to convince corporate America that China offered them a profit nirvana, and such was the intensity of the corporate lobbying in Washington that it took just seventeen months for Clinton to formally abandon his policy of linking trade to political reform.[11]

Much of the corporate lobbying for PNTR and accession to the WTO was done under the auspices of the US–China Business Council, but the late 1990s saw a proliferation of business organizations joining this lobby. The message from Beijing was clear: if American corporates wanted to operate profitably in China, then they needed to demonstrate that they were prepared to work for the attainment of China's strategic objectives – in this case, PNTR and WTO membership. The structure of China's economy, with the Party and the State firmly in control, meant that it was easy for officials to determine the level of market access and profitability that an individual company might enjoy in China.

It was not just multinational companies lobbying on behalf of China. Since access to Chinese officials was a crucial part of doing business in China, those who could secure that access had a valuable service to sell. Former US officials, who had befriended Chinese policymakers over the years, were well placed to make introductions. Such access would, of course, come with conditions attached, and clearly those that spoke out in favour of China's interests were more likely to have access to Chinese officials than those who criticized China. Henry Kissinger, through Kissinger Associates, was one such individual who continued to have access to Chinese decision-makers long after leaving office and who was able to monetize his contacts. While clearly all countries try to influence policy, particularly in the US, China was able to recruit an exceptionally powerful group of individuals and companies to fight their diplomatic battles against those who were more sceptical of China's motives.[12]

In the West, opposition to Chinese membership came from almost every segment of society except big business and high finance: labour, represented primarily by the trade unions; human rights activists and those who saw a moral dimension to foreign and trade policy; the conservative right; and environmentalists – in other words, almost everyone without a profit motive. Clearly, such an eclectic array of opponents was unlikely to produce one coherent set of arguments against PNTR and Chinese accession. Labour interests in the West that might once have admired communism ('Workers of the world unite!') now pointed to China's Dickensian labour laws and appalling working conditions. Apparently, in practice communism did not guarantee good working conditions. How could unskilled or semi-skilled workers in the developed world hope to compete in such a tussle? Globalization would continue to cause a 'race to the bottom' in terms of working conditions and workers rights. The wage disparity between China and the West would destroy employment prospects among trade union members.

The labour argument had some validity as far as it went. The issue was whether that segment of the population should be able to prevent society as a whole from benefiting from the lower cost of some goods that would be made available. Through the early 1980s unions in both the US and Europe had lost public support through their behaviour, which was often seen as stubborn, misplaced and against the broader public interest, and as a consequence they now suffered from a lack of credibility.

Some human rights advocates pointed out the abuses of the Chinese regime, which were brought to the world's attention by the events in Tiananmen Square in 1989 but which ran much deeper than that. The lack of an independent judicial system meant that the law was used to protect the state from the individual, not the individual from the state. The judiciary was simply an arm of the Party. These advocates also asked why engagement with China was the best solution to these injustices when isolating Cuba and Venezuela and the Soviet Union had been proposed as the best way to promote a free society there. Could not WTO membership be viewed as rewarding political repression, even tyranny? To both the trade unionist and the human rights activist, there was a strong stench of the profit motive and the influence of the corporate lobby about the argument for granting China PNTR.

Conservative opposition to PNTR revolved around ideology, geopolitics and economics. As a Cold War opponent, was it wise to allow China into US-dominated post-war institutions? Could they be trusted to play by the rules? China had a long track record of failing to live up to its obligation as far as protecting intellectual property rights was concerned. The trade relationship before WTO accession had been decidedly one-sided. Given the size of the country, China always had the potential to be a rival for regional if not global hegemony, but China had continually punched well below its weight. The status quo was perhaps the best the US and her allies could hope for and if change had to happen then surely the slower the better. If China wanted to take its rightful place at the top table of international institutions, surely they should be pressured to reform politics and the legal system first, while they were still economically weak. Was not WTO accession giving credence to an ideology that was the opposite of everything the US stood for? The economic benefits of trade with China from 1978 to 2000 had seemed to be largely one way: to China's benefit. How could the proponents of PNTR for China be so sure that WTO accession would change that? And if trade was going to make a communist-ruled China more prosperous, would it not be likely that a proportion of this new-found wealth would be used to challenge America's military suzerainty of Asia and beyond?

Many proponents of PNTR pointed out that China was not an expansionist country and that its sole foreign policy aims were the return of territory to the motherland: Hong Kong, Macau and Taiwan. Even though Tibet might be more contentious, at least to Chinese eyes, it was part of China and therefore not evidence of an expansionist bent to policy. If China's claims to Taiwan and Tibet boiled down to an issue of definition, however, then might not other historical claims also result in conflict? Such arguments perhaps also missed the point that China – although not expansionist by ideological calling – will need more oil, food, minerals and metals as her living standards approach those in the developed world, and securing these resources could bring her into conflict with other countries.

What seems clear from the political debate around unconditional economic engagement with China, both in the US and Europe, is that the lobby in favour of engagement with China was dominated by, and almost limited to, big business, and big business got its way. The politicians who were lobbied liked to dress up the arguments for closer economic engagement in the cloak of 'inducing change' but there is little evidence to support the idea that it was likely to happen, and we now know that it didn't. Foreign policy, it appears, was being driven by a narrow but powerful sectional interest and was not necessarily in the national interest. What is also clear is that China managed to drive a wedge between the EU, the US and other foreign powers, preventing a united front from being presented. The use of economic sanctions and favouritism, threats and cajoling during the accession process could have been a warning as to what to expect afterwards.

When the House of Representatives voted on PNTR on 24 May 2000 the Bill passed by 237 votes to 197 (roughly 55–45%). The Senate vote on granting China PNTR was carried 83–15 on 19 September 2000. By paving the way for China's WTO accession, Congress did away with its most important source of leverage over the Chinese regime: the ability to unilaterally and legally limit the trading relationship with China and impose economic sanctions on the country. Furthermore, they admitted a Communist totalitarian regime into the body that oversees the regulatory framework for global trade.

In many ways the decision can be said to have reflected the power of the corporate sector in the political process. Few voters, if any, had made free trade with China an electoral priority. There was no popular clamour for deepening economic relations with the People's Republic of China. Even the corporate lobby was divided, with the larger companies most likely to benefit from overseas operations and with the scale to at least potentially access the Chinese market supportive of PNTR, while smaller, domestic-orientated companies saw the dangers China posed. Expectations, however, were positive and high. China was expected to suffer some short-term pain as the economy was opened to competition, further redundancies at defunct SOEs would be unpopular but the longer-term benefits of permanent access to overseas markets, economic reform and a more transparent legal and regulatory system should have made that short-term pain worthwhile. The West, on the other hand, anticipated benefiting from rapid growth in service exports,

a narrowing of the trade imbalance and a China engaged construc-
tively on the global stage, playing by the rules of the multilateral
trading system and moving steadily but surely towards a more open,
pluralistic and free society governed by the rule of law. As President
Clinton had said: 'a one-way street'.

Chapter 2

Communist China's Post-WTO Economic Transformation

To get rich is glorious.
— Deng Xiaoping

THE YEARS THAT FOLLOWED CHINA'S accession to the WTO saw a marked acceleration in the pace of economic growth in China. The economic slowdown of the late 1990s, which had threatened to destabilize the regime with the potential for social chaos, was soon forgotten. Foreign direct investment (FDI) tripled in the first decade of the new millennium. Exports grew at an annual rate of nearly 30% during the first six years of WTO membership and China's share of world manufacturing was to rise fourfold, making it the largest manufacturer in the world and bringing ample employment opportunities for China's rapidly urbanizing population. If China had agreed to join the WTO on the promise of foreign investment, technology transfer and access to overseas markets for her exports, she was not disappointed. Furthermore, China seemed to control the temperature of competition that its cumbersome state-owned companies were subjected to and thus facilitated their survival. The worst of the anticipated economic risks failed to materialize while the promised benefits came thick and fast.

China had, of course, been achieving some spectacular economic growth well before the new millennium and its accession to the WTO. The growth of the 1980s and early 1990s was impressive and Western politicians would have given their eye-teeth to replicate these percentage changes. Chinese growth back then, however, was from a very low base. The adulation heaped on China's policymakers in the 1990s for guiding the economy to such tremendous levels of growth was not wholly undeserved, but it is widely appreciated that, if the starting point is low enough, spectacular percentage growth is easy to achieve if one makes a few simple policy choices in the right direction. Taiwan, Korea and Japan had to some extent shown the way. China's growth from the late 1970s to the early 1990s was impressive but not miraculous, and in fact by the middle of that decade much of the vigour had gone out of China's economic growth: reform had become more contentious and divisive.

It is easy in hindsight, knowing both the starting point and the destination, to think of China's economic rise as linear and inevitable, but it was neither. The Tiananmen Square massacre of 4 June 1989, the economic slowdown in China in the early 1990s, the accompanying industrial unrest and social dislocation and the devastating Asian financial crisis of 1997/98 all contributed to uncertainty as to which direction Chinese policy ought to or would take in the subsequent years. From today's vantage point, these events seem like mere hiccups, but they were momentous and potentially very destabilizing at the time. Without countervailing policies, the economic, social and political outcomes might have been very different. By the mid 1990s, with the easy gains from reform already made, the economy needed a new engine of growth, but one that would not lead to the kind of social instability so feared in China. The combination of the turmoil endured during the Mao years and the lack of political legitimacy for the regime made policymakers reluctant to take the tough decisions required to restructure the domestic economy. The answer to the policy dilemma of the late 1990s was to be found in export markets: the country was set to export its way out of both poverty and its political predicament.

If China's economic progress in the year running up to the turn of the century had been viewed with awe by much of the rest of the world, the growth in the first eight years of the new millennium was simply mind-boggling and truly unprecedented. The confidence that WTO accession gave to multinational companies to invest in China and the guarantee of access to developed markets for Chinese products produced the most spectacular trade boom of modern times. What began, or rather accelerated on a firmer footing, during this period was the largest labour market arbitrage in economic history. A population of 1.2 billion with a workforce of 750 million people and growing had formally joined the global trading system at a GDP per capita of about ⅓₀th of the advanced Western economies.

Most people would accept that WTO accession and export success speeded up China's development and meaningfully shortened the time frame it took for the country to become the regional economic superpower it is today. Perhaps the most important ramification of this was that China's economic rise was so swift and complete that it obviated the need for deepening economic reform and allowed economic progress to relieve the pressure for political change. Furthermore, it is debatable whether China would have reached middle-income status at all without the permanent access to world markets and the flows of FDI that WTO accession brought: improved export performance, along with its multiplier effect, may well have resulted – in just sixteen years – in an economy double the size it would otherwise have been. Plenty of emerging economies have made the right start and failed to see the process through to fruition. There was a serious risk in the mid 1990s that Chinese 'economic reformers' would lose the argument with the more economically conservative elements of the CPC and China would revert, if not to Maoism, at least to a more orthodox communist economic framework. Instead, it seems that economic success vindicated the actions of the CPC and validated the Party's monopoly of political life, not something that looked likely in 1978 when the reform process began.

Communist China's economic history can be divided into three very distinct periods. These are defined not only by the policies being pursued at the time, but also by the political imperative underlying those policies as well as the outcomes that were achieved. The disastrous three decades, for example, from 1949 to 1979, were marked by policies of ideologically driven collectivism, which drove the economy into the ground and produced a society barely capable of subsistence. This period represents the undeniable and complete failure of an economy dominated by collectivism and planning and isolated from technological progress. A political environment dominated by terror and an economic system devoid of the right incentives resulted in abject poverty. It was egalitarian only insofar as nobody had anything. It was from this low base, a position of complete and utter economic failure, that China began its climb to a position of economic hegemony of the Asian continent.

The launch of Deng Xiaoping's economic reforms in the late 1970s marked the start of China's economic recovery from the disaster of the preceding thirty years. In 1978, China's GDP, the total output of the economy, was a mere USD150 billion. The GDP of the US was USD2.6 trillion, which meant that while the per capita GDP of the US was already USD10,500 in the late 1970s in China it was just USD150. The average American was earning every week what the average Chinese person was earning in a year. Consequently, China's share of world GDP was a mere 1.5% despite its 20% share of the world population. The economic catastrophe of the post-war Maoist experiment meant that China was starting to open to the world economy from a level of subsistence not seen in the West for hundreds of years. In the late 1980s, not only did China have a cave-dwelling population, it was similar in size to that of the whole of the UK. In *China: The Next Economic Superpower*, William Overholt relates anecdotes from first-hand observations of families who used charcoal as a substitute for clothing (blackening their skin to hide their nakedness) or who would only go outside in thick fog or after dark for want of clothing.[13] If the West was worried about the rise of one-parent families, in China the concept of 'one-pants families', where clothes were worn in shifts, was often reported well into the 1990s. The country was desperately poor and resources hopelessly misallocated, but the consolation was that, as a result, small reforms could have a major and immediate impact and building a consensus to push through these changes was relatively easy. Reform was both efficacious and compatible with social harmony.

The Cultural Revolution and the Great Leap Forward had combined to set a base from which growth was easy to achieve. Agricultural reform, which incentivized farmers properly, produced food surpluses, and the labour shed from farming meant that rural industry was well supplied with workers. In 1978, per capita grain production, for example, was scarcely different from what it had been in 1950. Six years later it had risen by a third, largely due to the introduction of the Household Responsibility System that allowed farmers to reap the benefit of their own labour. The share of the workforce employed in agriculture stood at a staggering 70% in 1978 (to put this in context, the corresponding number in the US was about 3%). This started to fall, steadily, at a rate of one percentage point a year as reforms kicked in. This shift in employment did not necessarily entail a move to an urban environment, at least not during this transitional period of economic development. The pace of urbanization certainly accelerated after the 1978 reforms, before which it had been actively discouraged, but as late as 1995 only 29% of the Chinese population lived in cities. Agricultural reform thus led to rising productivity and farm incomes, which in turn fuelled demand for rural industrial products. Such easy productivity gains produced immediate and dramatic results, improving the everyday life of the population without the divisive elements that were to follow with later economic change. While the chaos of the Mao years had made economic growth easy to achieve in its immediate aftermath, it had also instilled in the Chinese population a fear of change and an overriding desire that, whatever economic arrangements were put in place, social harmony should be the paramount political goal.

By the late 1980s it was clear that economic reform was not going to be all plain sailing. Economic cycles were becoming volatile and China was struggling to master macroeconomic management. China's banking system served to channel the high rate of personal savings made by China's labourers into investments in SOEs. As one might expect in a centrally planned, communist economy, these enterprises were not particularly profit-minded. Employment was for life. Wages were unrelated to performance. As losses mounted up at these SOEs, it became increasingly clear that China's banking system was in fact bust. The restructuring of the SOE sector, it was publicly admitted, required about 30 million redundancies. The 'iron rice bowl', the system of corporate welfare that housed and fed the population, was in the process of being smashed, not out of a desire to wean the population off state dependency but because not to do so would potentially result in a Soviet-style collapse of the whole economic system. While necessary for the system's survival, the economic reforms of the late 1980s and early 1990s started to produce very noticeable losers as well as winners. Regional disparities in wealth started to become more obvious and inequality of income and wealth rose sharply. The rural–urban divide also widened. In addition, economic growth started to moderate dramatically from 1993 and the democracy movement seemed to provide ample evidence that the CPC was in danger of losing control.

Against this backdrop of increasingly mixed economic results, the Asian economic crisis of 1997 was a severe blow to the more reform-minded elements within the CPC. The crisis that began in mid 1997 and plunged the region into a deep recession brought an end to a long period of rapid economic development and growth. The crisis had many deep-rooted causes: corruption; an emphasis on investment for its own sake rather than the returns investment might generate; the prevalence of fixed-exchange-rate regimes that misallocated capital; and an unhealthy nexus between politicians, banks and plutocrats, to name but a few. The most obvious manifestation of the crisis, though, was the havoc that was reaped on currency markets by the flight of foreign capital. Furthermore, the sight of the IMF arriving in Asian capital cities and dictating economic and financial policy to sovereign governments was powerful ammunition for those in China who were against further economic liberalization. The apparent loss of national sovereignty, at least when things went wrong, that seemed to be a part and parcel of integration with the global economic system fuelled nationalist sentiments in China, as it also did in the worst-affected countries.

China managed to avoid the worst of the crisis. Her capital markets, such as they were, had not been open to foreign investors so they had no capital to withdraw. Trade relative to GDP was still relatively modest at 25% in 1997 and so the collapse in demand from her neighbours and the increased level of export competition from the newly devalued Asian currencies, while not insignificant, were bearable. One did not have to be a critic of economic reform, though, to see that had the Chinese economy been more integrated with the region, given the fragile nature of China's economic institutions, things could have been much worse. When regime change took place in Indonesia and the Suharto dynasty fell, there was more than a vague sense of 'there but for the grace of God go I' among the CPC hierarchy.

The economic reform process from 1978 through to the mid 1990s reflected the new political necessity: to deliver improving living standards to the Chinese people. The ideological *raison d'être* of the CPC had been replaced by a pragmatic one. The authority of the Party and any moral legitimacy the government may have had now depended on policy outcomes: delivering a higher standard of living year in year out. This was the new social contract.

Viewed from this perspective, the situation policymakers found themselves in during the tail end of the 1990s was particularly dire. While urban unemployment was running at between 12% and 15% in the late 1990s, in rural areas it is estimated that up to a third of workers were superfluous to requirements. Inflation that had risen as high as 30% in the early 1990s turned into deflation as overinvestment met subdued consumer demand. Precautionary savings skyrocketed as people feared for their jobs and their future.

The propensity of the Chinese to save rather than spend was to be a constant source of deficient domestic demand in the economy and at the core of China's need to export. The interest paid on bank deposits (the major form of savings for Chinese workers) collapsed to almost nothing. Corporate profits came under severe downward pressure, which in turn jeopardized the health of the state-run banking system. The CPC was in danger of failing to fulfil its side of the bargain. As protests and rioting became commonplace, policymakers needed a silver bullet – a panacea – that would drive growth forward in such a way as to avoid the tough and divisive decisions that could turn protest into regime change. If there was anything miraculous about the Chinese economy in the year 2000, twenty-two years into the economic reform process, it was just how small it was: how so many people and such a big land mass could produce so little.

There were many factors at play in the run-up to China's accession to the WTO at the end of 2001 but the overriding motivation for the Chinese was to improve export performance, attract foreign investment and facilitate technology transfer. These were the prerequisites for a new, vigorous, export-orientated growth drive. Of course, Chinese exports had been growing for a while, like everything else in China, fast off a low base. The actual speed and quantity of export growth that materialized, however, far exceeded even the most optimistic of expectations. The change of pace of growth in China's economy after WTO accession marks the event out as being a watershed that kick-started a new era in her economic development. Export success went hand in hand with deploying China's high savings into manufacturing capacity. That in turn fuelled employment growth, urbanization, infrastructure investment and overall GDP growth.

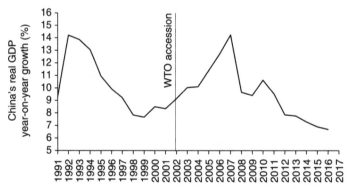

Figure 1. WTO accession led to a rapid reacceleration of China's GDP growth in the early 2000s. *Source*: World Bank open database.

Writing at the end of 1997, four years before China's entry into the WTO but when the accession process was well advanced and the political debate in full swing, the World Bank produced a report entitled 'China 2020'.[14] Not surprisingly it was a report strongly in favour of a policy of engagement between China and the rest of the world. In the report the authors argue that China's growth would provide an opportunity for the world, not a threat, but they observed that trade had become a more sensitive and politicized issue than when the US rose to dominate global trade and when Japan enjoyed its rapid economic ascent on the back of export growth. 'By 2020 China could be the world's second largest exporter and importer' the report states and points out that such rapid growth would not be without precedent as both the US (1870–1913) and Japan (1952–95) underwent similarly sharp periods of growth in trade as they engaged with the world.

In fact, China overtook America as the largest exporting nation in 2007 just ten years after the World Bank's report. Six years of nearly 30% growth from 2001 to 2007 compounded to drive a fivefold increase in the US-dollar-denominated value of China's exports, taking China from seventh globally to the number one spot. This achievement was indeed without precedent and clearly confounded the economists at the international institutions who had not seen it coming. China's exports in 2007, USD1.2 trillion, were larger than its whole economy had been in 2000.

The 'China 2020' report also made predictions about China's likely future GDP growth trajectory. Naturally enough, this was done through some scenario analysis revolving around assumed levels of productivity growth and the savings rate and hence capital accumulation. Rightly, the report pointed out that, with time, diminishing marginal returns on capital, demographics and a more efficient base would result in a slowing of the pace of growth. Given the slowdown that China had seen in growth from 1993 to 1997 it would have seemed sensible at the time to assume some of those diminishing returns had indeed already arrived. Chinese real GDP growth had been running in the mid-teens in the early 1990s but had been declining steadily to the 7–9% range, where it oscillated between 1997 and 2000. Back in 1997, an extrapolation of this trend would lead one to conclude that a 4–8% GDP growth rate through to 2020 was a reasonable range for an estimate – albeit perhaps a wide one encompassing many variations in contributing factors.

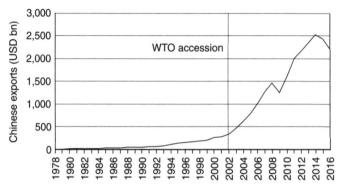

Figure 2. WTO accession facilitated an unprecedented growth in China's exports at the expense of domestic manufacturing in the West and other rival exporters. *Source*: WTO.

From 2000 to 2008, however, GDP growth in China reaccelerated dramatically as export penetration reenergized the economy. Naturally, since one thing led to the other, the failure to anticipate the dramatic and unprecedented pace of export growth meant the authors dramatically underestimated the pace of GDP growth too. While real GDP growth averaged about 10.5% between 1992 and 2000 on a declining trend, between 2000 and 2008 it also averaged 10.5% but on a rising trend. WTO accession, it seems, brought China at least another seven years or so of supercharged GDP growth. In US dollar nominal terms, the growth in this second phase of development was even more spectacular than in the first, rising to a 15% compound annual growth rate (CAGR) in the post-WTO accession era from 10% beforehand.

Further compounding the miscalculation of the speed of China's rise in relative importance in the world, the World Bank and other forecasters also misjudged the pace of growth in the rest of the world, which, relative to their expectations, has been disappointing since the turn of the century. Hence the relative importance of China – not just in economic terms, but also, as a direct result, in geopolitical and military terms – has risen much faster than was envisaged by proponents of a policy of unconditional engagement. China's rapid expansion coincided with a period of economic stagnation in the rest of the world relative to previous growth trends. The failure of expert forecasters to predict the scale of change WTO accession would bring is in itself evidence of just how dramatic a watershed the event was. Membership paved the way for the ruthless and well-executed pursuit of an export-orientated, mercantilist growth model. While domestic economic reforms continued up to a point, the prime mover of China's economic transformation was now an exporting industrial complex. The economic development model, while based around overseas market access, depended also on cheap labour, an undervalued and fixed exchange rate and a high savings rate to fund the investment in new capacity and the associated infrastructure. This was pursued with the single-mindedness of the national project that it was. The consequence was a dramatic acceleration in China's growth rate that provided the much-needed employment opportunities, through migration, for both the urban unemployed and the rural underemployed. In doing so the export engine bought time and space for policymakers to push forward with administrative reform while avoiding the potential for social disintegration and obviating the need to move more fully towards a market economy.

From a GDP level of USD1.2 trillion in 2000, China's GDP reached USD11.2 trillion in 2016. China's share of global GDP rose fourfold from 3.5 to 14%. By 2016, per capita GDP in China had reached USD8,100 or 80% of the world average, making the country a middle-income economy. In a decade and a half China was transformed from a low-income emerging economy into a global economic superpower. The difference between a 15% compound annual growth rate achieved for the sixteen years following WTO accession and the 10% achieved before accession may not sound very dramatic, but such is the power of compounding that an economy that grows at 15% for sixteen years becomes twice as large as one that grows at 10% for sixteen years with the same starting point. In other words, in 2016, the Chinese economy was twice as large as experts had forecast it would be in their most optimistic scenario back in 2000.

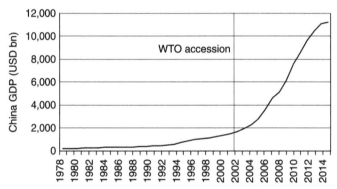

Figure 3. Unanticipated export success has led to a Chinese economy twice as large as might otherwise have been the case. *Source*: World Bank open database.

What is remarkable about China's rise to dominance of global trade is the speed with which it happened. At the end of World War II, America's hegemony of the global economy was complete. The British Empire was being disbanded; Germany was divided and destroyed; Japan needed rebuilding from scratch; and China was gripped by civil war. As late as 1969, the US with just 6% of the world's population accounted for 37% of global GDP and 13% of global exports. Towards the end of the 1960s, Japan began to expand exports rapidly in what at the time seemed like an economic miracle. However, it took twenty years for Japan's share of world exports to reach double digits, peaking at 10% in 1986, where it plateaued. The market share grab was dramatic and for a country of 100 million people in 1970 – just 3% of the world's population – the importance of Japan to international trade far outweighed its size. Yet this was nothing compared to China's achievements in the 2000s.

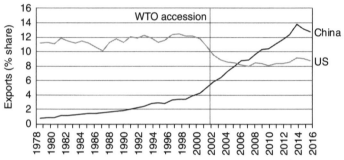

Figure 4. China and US share of global exports (%) 1978–2016.
Source: WTO.

In 1978, China had a 1% market share of world exports and they did not reach 2% until 1991. At this juncture, as FDI in China began, the growth rate accelerated and market share doubled over the next decade through to WTO accession in 2001. Even at this juncture, though, China was an also-ran in global trade, ranking seventh, below Canada. Japan's share of exports, despite (or perhaps because of) its 'lost decade', was 50% larger than China's in 2001 and the US share was nearly three times China's. In the six years after China's WTO accession, however, something quite extraordinary happened. China's export values grew just under five times in six years, a 29% compound annual growth rate, taking them from roughly USD250 billion to USD1.2 trillion, catapulting China into first place in the ranking of exporting nations. A country that at the start of that period had accounted for just 4%

of global GDP was now the world's most prolific exporter. In fact, China's exports in 2007 were about the same as its GDP had been in 2000. China's imports, other countries' exports to China, also grew massively, although, importantly, not as fast. China's current account surplus, the narrowing of which had been one of the key arguments put forward by proponents of PNTR in the US, rose from a fairly consistent 2% of GDP before WTO to a record 10% of GDP.

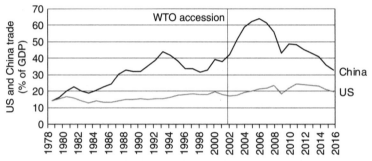

Figure 5. For a large economy, China remains highly dependent on trade. *Source*: WTO and World Bank open database.

Total trade (imports and exports) rose from 10% of China's GDP in 1978 to 40% in 2001 to 65% of China's GDP in 2006. To put that in perspective, Japan's ratio of trade to GDP did not exceed 30% during its ascendency in the 1980s and the US's marginally exceeded 25% of GDP only recently and fleetingly. In other words, during the transition period in China's economic development (before WTO accession), trade became a relatively normally sized contributor to economic activity, albeit at the higher end of the normal range. During the growth surge inspired by WTO accession, however, China's trade dependence more than doubled from the normal range for a large economy. Economic growth become almost exclusively dependent on trade and its associated investment in infrastructure and capacity: the trade multiplier.

The major factor behind the rapid rise in China's exports, other than secure market access, was the cost advantage that came from low labour costs and what some observers would describe as Dickensian labour laws. Totalitarian states, even communist ones, are not renowned for their protection of workers' rights and China was no exception. Labour, however, had always been both abundant and cheap in China but the real rise to middle-income status and hence regional economic dominance came after WTO accession. One explanation for the dramatic explosion in China's trade was the inflow of FDI following WTO accession. Rightly or wrongly, Chinese membership of the WTO gave multinational companies the confidence that they were dealing with a rules-based system of regulation and governance. This enticed foreign companies to set up manufacturing facilities in China, which had been the recipient of a modest net flow of FDI since the early 1990s. In the decade to 2000, the net inflow amounted to about USD300 billion but in the following decade this more than tripled to over USD1 trillion.

As we have seen, multinational companies were really the only constituency in the West to lobby hard for Chinese membership of the WTO. President Clinton had been elected on a campaign promise to link China's trade access to the US market explicitly to measurable improvements in human rights. This was in stark contrast to the previous administration's almost ambivalent attitude to human rights issues that was on display in the aftermath of the Tiananmen Square massacre. Organizations such as the US–China Business Council had lobbied hard for Congress to approve PNTR for China and once China was in the WTO multinational companies wasted no time in investing there. Even in the late 1990s 'foreign invested' companies accounted for about 40% of China's exports but this proportion rose steadily towards 60% after accession. One must be cautious of reading too much into this number as many foreign investments were in fact Chinese capital rerouted through offshore havens such as the BVI and Hong Kong to take advantage of tax breaks and other incentives but, even so, multinational companies clearly accounted for a very substantial proportion of the exports coming out of China.

Work by Michael Enright has highlighted the crucial but under-appreciated role that FDI played in facilitating the speed and magnitude of China's economic ascent.[15] The cumulative total of FDI into China now amounts to about USD1.6 trillion. While this is small in comparison to the size of domestic investment, it has been highly effective. If one includes the knock-on impact of this foreign investment on local employment and therefore spending, supply chains and distribution, Enright concludes that between 2009 and 2013 one-third of Chinese GDP was the result of investment by foreign-invested enterprises. Furthermore, 27% of Chinese employment can be traced to the direct and indirect consequences of FDI. Such numbers demonstrate the degree to which China's rise was facilitated by and continues to depend on not just the lobbying efforts of multinational corporations to get China into the WTO but their subsequent investments.

Foreign companies were not the only institutions investing heavily to take advantage of China's new market access and under-valued labour. The high savings rate in China is one of the factors that marks the country out from its Western trading partners. A history of uncertainty, chaos and turmoil means that, culturally, some would argue, the Chinese are prone to save. The economic reforms of the 1980s removed much of the social safety net or 'iron rice bowl' and further increased precautionary saving. As income levels rose, the Chinese showed a very high propensity to save income in excess of that required to provide the most basic of lifestyles, but, until recently, there was a limited choice of savings products available in China. China's financial institutions, which gather savings and invest them in companies, were and still are largely state owned. At the core of China's financial system are the big four state-owned banks that dominate deposit taking in the country, and therefore the savings industry generally, and they control the lion's share of bank lending.

At the heart of China's economic reform programme was a simple truth: for the CPC to remain in power it had to start delivering improved living standards to the population at large. The economic failure of the 1950s and 1960s would ultimately result in the demise of the Party if it were repeated and not reversed. State control of savings and investment was, naturally for the communists, seen as key to ensuring that the prosperity created by reforms and international market access was harnessed in such a way as to consolidate and cement Party power rather than challenge it.

State-owned financial institutions pursuing political goals behave in very different ways to profit-maximizing ones responding to the desires of shareholders. The key priority in making loans is to attain national objectives (in this case, export market share) or politically dictated local goals. These could range from domination of an industry at a global level, to promoting a technology to give China independence in a particular sphere, to promoting employment in a particular city. Investment objectives might be wide ranging, but they are determined by the CPC or a cadre within it and ultimately have a political end. Very low on the list of concerns is whether or not a borrower can repay the loan or service the interest costs. Advancement through the ranks of the CPC is often dependent on achieving specific growth-orientated goals at a parochial level. Control over the savings pool to facilitate investment and achieve economic targets was therefore a necessity for political promotion. Observers who hoped WTO accession would result in a rapid opening of the financial industry probably misread this situation. Too much competition for savings along more market-orientated lines would emasculate officialdom.

With labour abundant and cheap, and with capital purchases financed by loans from state banks that were forgiving when it came to payment terms, China's corporations were perfectly placed to win global market share at the expense of other players. The trade statistics show that they did and are the mirror image of China's success in capturing global share in manufacturing. In 1997 on the eve of the Asian crisis, China had a 6% share of global manufacturing (measured in terms of value added). This did not change much in the years running up to WTO membership but in the first twelve years after WTO accession China's market share quadrupled to 24%, overtaking both the US and the EU to become the largest manufacturer of goods in the world. Not far off half the growth in the first fifteen years of this century in global manufacturing was accounted for by China.

There are those that argue that China's growth was not as export orientated as many of the numbers show. In 2008, a time when exports were 40% of GDP, the value added of those exports was just 10% of GDP: China was importing inputs and exporting outputs with the value added measuring the importance to GDP. This of course was a function of the manufactured nature of Chinese exports, but it misses the point that, along with the actual exports, a large part of China's growth was coming from the accoutrements of trade: port infrastructure, ships, containers, the building of factories and roads required by the exporting complex. The acid test came when the global economy slowed in 2008/9 and China's economy hit the proverbial brick wall. The size of the fiscal and monetary intervention required to pull the economy back from the brink was a stark testimony to how dependent growth had been on exports. True, the earlier recession of 2001/2 had a more modest impact on Chinese growth but that was before the rapid rise in China's export penetration into the global economy.

From a global perspective, two factors mark out this second, post-WTO accession period of growth as being starkly different from the first period: first, China's contribution to global GDP growth in the period from 2000 to 2016 was staggering. The USD10 trillion of growth in China's GDP accounted for nearly a quarter of all growth in the world over the sixteen-year period. In the post-crisis part of this period (2008–16), 6.6 out of the 12.1 trillion dollars of global growth came from China: her GDP grew from USD4.6 trillion in 2008 to USD11.2 trillion in 2016 while global GDP grew from USD63.4 trillion to USD75.5 trillion. China therefore accounted for over half of global growth. Never has the world economy been so driven by such a relatively small weighted economy. As things currently stand, as a driver of global growth, China has usurped the US as the most important economy in the world, even though its economy is only 60% of the size of the US in nominal terms.

The second factor that was very different in the post-WTO period was that, while in the first period America's share of global GDP rose slightly, in the second period it fell sharply. Up until 2000 there was nothing to suggest that China's rapid economic growth was coming at the expense of American hegemony. Sure, China's share of global GDP doubled off a low base but America's rose too. After 2000, China's rise looked increasingly as if it was undermining US dominance. From 2000 to 2016 America's share of global GDP fell from 31% to 25% while China's share rose from 3.6% to nearly 15%. More than half of China's share gain came at the expense of the US. The direction of travel may well have been inevitable, but the speed of the transition was not and was down to Western acquiescence with China's mercantile behaviour. The narrowing of the gap between the economies of China and the US is being reflected in China's growing geopolitical influence, particularly in the Asia–Pacific region but also beyond. If the collapse of the Soviet Union led observers to believe that Western liberalism would soon be the lone ideology in the world, the rise of China has proved them wrong.

China now finds itself as the key driver of global growth, a regional economic hegemon, and the largest manufacturer and exporter in the world. Yet it got there in large part, not by harnessing market forces to allocate resources efficiently, nor by liberating its population from the intellectual monopolizing influence of the CPC. China's rise was achieved by the adoption of an economic nationalism that harnessed some aspects of a market economy, to pursue societal goals set by central government. To what extent China's accession to the WTO facilitated this remarkable rise in economic power is contested by some but to a large extent the results speak for themselves. It certainly provided an environment in which both foreign investors and the Chinese themselves felt secure in investing in China's export sector. What is not debatable is that, sixteen years after accession, the Chinese economy was about twice as large as it was forecast to be: the growth rate accelerated dramatically after accession and China achieved unprecedented success in penetrating overseas markets, taking market share in manufacturing. The CPC, it appears, got everything it wanted out of WTO accession and capitalized on the opportunities handsomely. The US corporate lobby saw profits rise by outsourcing production and exploiting the labour arbitrage opportunity. As for the trade deficit, instead of falling it exploded, and the fabled profits to be made from the 1.2 billion Chinese consumers (1.4 billion now) remain for the most part a work in progress. The transition to a market economy, even one with distinct Chinese characteristics, was never completed, let alone the move to a pluralistic, democratized society. The export model was so successful it obviated the need for deeper economic and political reform. 'A one-way street' as President Clinton called it, but not in the direction he had anticipated.

Chapter 3

The Triumph of Mercantilist China

Mercantilism: The economic theory that trade generates wealth and is stimulated by the accumulation of profitable balances, which a government should encourage by means of protectionism.

— Oxford English Dictionary

By joining the WTO, China is not simply agreeing to import more of our products; it is agreeing to import one of democracy's most cherished values: economic freedom. The more China liberalizes its economy, the more fully it will liberate the potential of its people – their initiative, their imagination, their remarkable spirit of enterprise. And when individuals have the power, not just to dream but to realize their dreams, they will demand a greater say.

— President Bill Clinton[16]

I T IS AN INTERESTING IDEA: that the importation and exportation of goods and services does not happen without a similar trade in 'values'. In a speech at Johns Hopkins University, President Clinton argued that China's accession to the WTO would change

China beyond recognition. China was agreeing to import not only American goods and services but, as a result, economic freedom. In this case, so the argument ran, where economic freedom went, prosperity would follow, and where people were prosperous they would demand a greater say in politics. A market economy, democracy and liberalism would inevitably, given time, follow on from where trade led.

China's SOEs were notoriously inefficient. The incentive structures were perverse. They existed to employ and provide security to a population lacking more productive employment opportunities. At the time, they employed upwards of 150 million workers and a third of them were thought to be unnecessary. By exposing such institutions to outside competition, the frontiers of the state could be rolled back. New, private enterprises would take their place and a huge source of Communist Party patronage and control would be undermined. By exposing the inefficiency of the command economy's institutions, they would be forced to close or reform:

> Now people are leaving those firms [the SOEs], and when China joins the WTO, they will leave them faster. The Chinese government no longer will be everyone's employer, landlord, shopkeeper and nanny all rolled into one. It will have fewer instruments, therefore, with which to control people's lives. And that may lead to very profound change.[17]

It is clear from this speech and many others by proponents of granting China PNTR (and so paving the way for China's WTO accession) that the assumption was that the political and economic institutions of China were too weak to survive exposure to the West through trade. No one seemed to anticipate that our political and economic institutions might be stress-tested too, that the West in general, and the US in particular, would be on the receiving end of an ideological exchange, and not just a source of values. After all, the thesis was that when goods change hands across the border of a country, so do values. And the evidence was then, and even more clearly is now, that China has been better at exporting than at importing. Might that be applicable to the exchange in 'values' as well as the exchange of goods? Clinton had promised that exposure to Western goods and hence ideas would bring about political change in China and help drive the country towards a pluralistic, free and open society. Few considered how the liberal democracies of the West might be affected in the same way through trade with China.

If democratic capitalism has a moral foundation it is that, while economic outcomes may not be equal, they are fair. Participants enjoy the fruits of their own labour and enterprise and they exchange those rewards in a free market with others. Remuneration is earned in a competitive marketplace for labour and is spent in a competitive marketplace for goods and services. Savings become capital and are allocated to where the returns are expected to be highest. Outcomes are not determined by politicians or bureaucrats or the preferences of a collective body but by the individual action of millions of participating individuals that together make up 'the market'. Prices act as the balancing factor to ration anything that is scarce, bringing supply and demand into equilibrium, sending signals to market participants that enable them to adjust their behaviour accordingly. A liberal democratic society is a bottom-up construct. The goals of the society are simply the aggregate goals of the individuals that make up the society. American or European democracies do not have a national economic plan, or at least their governments do not. A national economic plan implies a national economic objective. The level of consumption or savings in the economy is determined by market forces. The pattern of production and consumption reflects the demands of the consumers, not the plans of the bureaucracy. State control of the means of production is incompatible with individualism and liberalism. In recent years, particularly since 1945, the UK, continental Europe and even America have moved further away from this ideal than some would wish, but even the mixed economy of the social democrat is still far closer to the liberal 'ideal' than it is to the political economy of communist China.

Among those in the West who do not subscribe to the liberal, moral argument for capitalism in its purest form, the majority believe that the market economy can redeem itself by virtue of its results. It fulfils a utilitarian purpose by producing wealth far in excess of that produced by alternative economic systems, which can then be harnessed for collective objectives. The battle between these two views of the market economy – a moral necessity and guarantor of the supremacy of the individual over the state, or a necessary tool for the creation of the wealth a society needs – has dominated post-war politics in the West.

In communist China, the Party, the nation and the government are one, an unholy trinity if you will, and the interests of the individual are subordinate to those of the Party. Society is a top-down construct. Incidentally, this is not just as a result of communist ideology. Asian philosophy has a long history, predating the foreign import of communism, that emphasized societal goals over those of the individual, as of course did pre-mercantile Europe. In the political economy of China, as it existed in 1978, nearly all factors of production – land, labour and capital (of which there was very little) – were employed through the agency of entities either owned or controlled by the state. The planning process was central to policy and all policy was pursued to the end of achieving national objectives. The abject failure of this economic system, and the consequence that it threatened systemic collapse and the loss of Communist Party power, was the motivation for a rethink. The changes that were introduced by Deng Xiaoping were aimed at improving the results of the system to make the national objectives achievable. What the Chinese authorities were attempting was to harness some of the incentive structures of capitalism to make a totalitarian, communist economy more successful. It was only by producing better results that the CPC stood a chance of maintaining power and this became even more evident when the Soviet Union collapsed. The CPC was therefore prepared to replace a dogmatic approach to economics with a new pragmatism to facilitate their survival.

The reforms, such as they were, did not change the structure of the political economy of China beyond recognition, even if they had the effect of very dramatically changing the performance of the economy. Capital was allocated almost exclusively by state-controlled banks. Minsheng Bank, which wasn't founded until 1996, was the first privately owned bank in communist China, but even today, forty years after the reform process began, and seventeen years after WTO accession, with its promise of foreign access to the capital markets, the big four state-owned banks and the two major policy banks still control most of the lending.

The commanding heights of the economy were still state controlled in 2000. According to Bill Clinton:

> Nearly 60 percent of the investment, and 80 percent of all business lending, still goes towards state-owned dinosaurs that are least likely to survive in the global economy and most likely to be vulnerable to corruption.

What is perhaps telling is that, despite the rise of the private sector, there had not (and still has not) been a diminution in the importance of China's economic planning. Private enterprise is a means of facilitating the achievement of national goals; it is not a goal in itself. Government policy and planning are still omnipotent and price, as a mechanism for rationing or signalling, is subservient.

Every five years the CPC leadership presents the next Five-Year Plan, and the Plan for the period 2016–21 is the thirteenth such document.[18] It runs to eighty chapters and 60,000 Chinese characters but in addition to the overarching plan there are separate detailed plans applicable at the ministry and industry level: the 13th Five-Year Plan for the Development of Emerging Strategic Industries, for example, or the 13th Five-Year Market Supervision Plan, or the Civilian Explosives Industry Development Plan. The level of detail and the granularity of the targets are either astounding or incredulous depending on your perspective. China will increase the number of patents filed from 6.3 per 10,000 people in 2015 to 12 per 10,000 people in 2020. China's global ranking for the number of citations in international science and technology publications will rise from 4th to 2nd if the plan is successful, and the proportion of the total population holding a scientific degree will rise from 6.2% to 10%. Partly because of these targets being reached, the contribution to overall growth in the economy made by science and technological advances will rise from 55.3% to 60%. There are plans for the internationalization of small- and medium-sized businesses, bioindustry, new electric vehicles and for promoting mass innovation. The Five-Year Plan contains targets for everything from urbanization rates, land use, poverty reduction and educational attainment to life expectancy and the utilization of the ocean.

Under international trade law, the scope for applying anti-dumping duties to exports from a non-market economy (NME) is greater than exports from a market economy. Anti-dumping duties are import taxes designed to compensate for some unfair advantage gained by the exporter that has enabled them to sell produce at below market price. They constitute the main sanction and form of redress available to a country that has suffered from unfair trade practices. The rationale for distinguishing between market and non-market economies should be obvious, if prices are set by the state, not the market, a non-market economy could wreak havoc on a market economy by subsidizing, or otherwise artificially lowering, the selling price of a good to gain a strategic foothold in a market or to obliterate a domestic industry in another country. By purloining the resources of the state for such a specific purpose, an NME could produce economic outcomes that would be unfair and debilitating to specific segments of a market-driven economy. A problem for policymakers arises from the definitions of 'market' and 'non-market' economies. An additional problem arises from the fact that, as intellectual fashions change, and indeed as governments change in a democracy, they are dealing with a dynamic process. Would a UK run by Jeremy Corbyn for ten years, for example, be a market or a non-market economy? It certainly would not be the same economy as one run by Margaret Thatcher. Being a democracy is not the same as being a market economy. Membership of the EU is dependent on being a market economy as defined by the EU. The US recognized Russia as a market economy in 2002. Hence, one can see the scope for a huge amount of political expediency in the definitions applied in differing circumstances as diplomatic and economic leverage is applied, but from an economic and moral perspective the underlying need for a definition does not change. The acid test remains: will trade between the market economy and the non-market one produce outcomes that can be deemed unfair due to state interference?

In reality, all economies are mixed to some degree, a combination of market-driven and state-driven outcomes. What matters is where on this spectrum an economy is positioned and its ability to inflict damage. That is determined by the areas of economic activity into which the state reaches and the economy's size. To take an extreme example, it is unclear that a laissez-faire approach in the international trade in armaments is either achievable or desirable. In fact, it is clear that it is not: the primary purpose of the industry is to defend the nation against hostile acts from other nations. The level of state involvement in the industry is simply too high to pretend that companies can operate independently from government and on an equal and fair footing with foreign competitors. Apart from anything else, the state, or similarly aligned states, are the monopoly buyer of the product (we hope) and they will spend taxpayers' money in a different way to a profit-maximizing or utility-maximizing buyer with a more narrowly defined set of criteria. A government, particularly a democratic one that has to be responsive to an electorate, will take into account not just the efficacy of the equipment, the cost and strategic issues pertaining to maintenance and operational efficiency but most likely employment potential in a home market (in times of war, access to foreign-made equipment may be limited), the political alignment of any foreign supplier and the likelihood or not of the same equipment being sold to a potential adversary, and so on. More importantly, any company or individual who engineers a strong comparative advantage in the manufacture of weaponry through innovation will most likely find that their own government severely limits their ability to monetize it through international sales! No set of international trade rules could hope to govern such a complex and politicized set of transactions and anyone hoping for a morally defensible and equitable economic outcome for the workers, owners or other stakeholders in companies involved in the manufacture of armaments will be disappointed. Does the existence of state involvement in the defence industry nullify the positive impact to be had from free trade in other areas among countries or make an economy non-market? Surely not.

Historically, there have been many countries that have joined multilateral trading systems (GATT and WTO) at times when their economies have been indisputably non-market, Yugoslavia, Poland, Romania and Hungary being good examples. In each case the economy of the joining country was small, trade was limited and their ability to severely distort the allocation of resources or the equity of outcomes in market economies almost non-existent. Tellingly, in each case, there was a political imperative to entice the country away from the Soviet sphere of influence and so the emphasis was on adjusting the rules of the trading system to accommodate the new country. The political gain to the West of allowing these NMEs into the trading system was far in excess of any collateral damage to their own economies.

In the WTO era, though, with the collapse of the Soviet Union, and the accession of a large number of former Soviet satellite states, the emphasis was not on changing the rules of the trading system but instead on changing the economic structure of the joining economy through imposing obligations on the accession country. These could pertain to, say, privatization, foreign exchange policy or industrial policy. These obligations were designed to facilitate the transition from a non-market to a market economy, often over a stipulated time-frame.

What had become increasingly clear during the evolution of the multilateral trading system was that while quantifiable barriers to free trade, such as tariffs and quotas, were relatively easy to legislate against, the subtler obstacles to creating a level playing field – state subsidies, industrial policy or simply bureaucratic impediments to free movement – were far more difficult to solve. The rule book of the WTO was not designed to facilitate the integration of a country not committed to free trade with a free market one, even if such a task were possible. The WTO was intended to supervise trade between economies that shared market characteristics or were on a politically driven path towards adopting such characteristics. It could perhaps regulate trade between countries that actually wanted free and fair trade, but where a country was determined to obstruct market access through less obvious barriers, the WTO's rules and enforcement mechanisms would be left wanting.

What clearly stood out about China was the potential size of its economy, and therefore the very dramatic influence it could exert on the global trading system. Indeed, when it finally acceded to the WTO it was the seventh largest exporter in the world. Its track record of expanding export share had been impressive in the years running up to the conclusion of the membership process, although from a low base the impact of this success on the economies of the rest of the world was still limited. However, two other factors could have featured far more than they did in policy deliberations. First, unlike in Eastern Europe, where the collapse of the Soviet political system and its associated communist regimes had led to an apparent ideological conversion to democracy and free market economics, in China there had been no such political collapse nor a change in economic thinking. Both the pace and scale of economic change in China was being controlled by the CPC. It was pragmatic not dogmatic, and it was never intended, at least not by those in control, to lead to political change. The second issue, which appears to have been either underappreciated or brushed under the carpet, was China's already dubious track record of compliance with existing obligations that had been placed on her as conditions for her pre-existing trading relationships.

On 11 December 2001, when China finally acceded to the WTO, the multilateral trading system unexpectedly changed beyond recognition. What had been predominantly an organization for overseeing freer trade among countries with similar economic structures changed first into an organization prepared to help facilitate the transition of former communist countries to market-orientated ones. Now it was being charged with implementing a set of rules and agreements between its member countries and a communist totalitarian state with no ideological commitment to a market-orientated economy at all. Among the optimists looking at this situation was Supachai Panitchpakdi, a former director-general of WTO:

> The WTO will set out rules for a market-based economy. It
> will eliminate unfair treatment that now favours state-owned

firms and discriminates against foreign companies and local entrepreneurs.[19]

This attitude was quite prevalent, and shared by the President of the United States, among others. WTO rules meant that China would have the rule of law. The obligations China had taken on through its WTO membership would trump domestic policy and so China could be thought of as another transition economy, albeit a rather big one.

China's success in quadrupling its market share in global manufacturing and in growing the US dollar value of its exports fivefold over the seven years after WTO accession strongly suggests Chinese diplomats got the better of their counterparts in the negotiation of the terms of their accession. Alternatively, of course, the success could have been because the terms of the accession agreement were flouted.[20] Or the success could have come because, whenever a nation deploys a system of state capitalism in export markets against opponents who are playing by the rules of a non-interventionist system, it's the state capitalists who will win.

At the end of 2017, sixteen years after China joined the WTO and forty years after Deng Xiaoping began his tentative economic reforms, the US Department of Commerce undertook an assessment of China's economy with a view to ascertaining if it should change its legal status from non-market economy to market economy:

> The Department of Commerce ('Department') concludes that China is a non-market economy (NME) country because it does not operate sufficiently on market principles to permit the use of Chinese prices and costs for purposes of the Department's antidumping analysis. The basis for the Department's conclusion is that the state's role in the economy and its relationship with markets and the private sector results in fundamental distortions in China's economy.[21]

The study looked at six factors in making its determination:

> The Department take into account (1) the extent to which the currency of the foreign country is convertible into the currency of other countries; (2) the extent to which wage rates in the foreign country are determined by free bargaining between labor and management; (3) the extent to which joint ventures or other investments by firms of other foreign countries are permitted in the foreign country; (4) the extent of government ownership or control of the means of production; (5) the extent of government control over the allocation of resources and over the price and output decisions of enterprises; and (6) such other factors as the administering authority considers appropriate.

Because Chinese citizens are not free to exchange their RMB-denominated savings, say bank deposits, into US dollars or other foreign currencies, Chinese banks can offer lower interest rates on these savings – their customers have little or no alternative.[22] Furthermore, the government has recently adopted various policies – including, for example, requiring prior government approval for overseas corporate acquisitions – aimed at preventing the capital account from running into uncontrollable deficit. Even at a more mundane level, spending by Chinese tourists overseas is controlled and subject to restriction. This obviously limits the growth of outbound tourism and denies some of China's trading partners who have a comparative advantage in offering tourism services what is due to them. The very existence of China's foreign exchange reserves is evidence that, at times, albeit not so recently, the People's Bank of China (the central bank) has intervened on a gargantuan scale to prevent the renminbi from appreciating. Such a policy has an obvious and pervasive influence on the allocation of resources within the economy and in particular on the relative pricing of exports vis-à-vis imports.

It is hard to disagree with the conclusions reached in many of the other areas examined by the Department of Commerce. The foreign investment regime is still subject to many limitations and prohibitions. The Department points out:

> The OECD, in its FDI Regulatory Restrictiveness Index, has continually ranked the Chinese government's foreign investment regime as one of the most restrictive in the world, even after some initial improvements following China's accession to the WTO. In 2016, the OECD FDI Regulatory Restrictiveness Index ranked China 59th out of 62 countries in 2016, just after Myanmar and five times as restrictive as the country average.

Indeed, taking into account the additional qualitative barriers to foreign investment, it could be argued that China has made miniscule progress during its WTO membership on this front. The rule seems to have been that foreign investment in export-orientated industries has been welcomed with open arms but that investment has been severely restricted when it's been aimed at taking domestic market share in industries such as financial or corporate services where Western companies enjoy a comparative advantage.

SOEs continue to play a major role in the Chinese economy. In banking, state banks continue to dominate deposit gathering and commercial lending. The telecoms industry is almost entirely controlled by the three SOEs: China Mobile, China Unicom and China Telecom. The market leaders in the domestic auto industry are joint ventures between foreign manufacturers and SOEs. The major commercial airlines are state owned, as is the commercial aircraft manufacturing industry. Transportation, infrastructure, healthcare and the energy industry are also all dominated by SOEs. Overall, if National Bureau of Statistics data is to be believed,

SOEs account for about half the investment taking place in China even now after forty years of 'transition'.

SOEs play multiple roles in the Chinese economy. They are part employment agency, soaking up surplus labour and thus distorting the labour market, although this role has been diminishing in importance lately. They are instruments of government policy that help to achieve strategic goals relating to, for example, production targets and also stabilization policy. They are expected to invest when required to do so and to rein in investment if required. But more than anything they allow the CPC and the government to control the means of production. Indeed, in a retrograde step, the CPC, as opposed to the government through the State-owned Assets Supervision and Administration Commission of the State Council (SASAC), is being formally written into the memorandum and articles of listed SOEs.[23]

The visible manifestations of China's economy have changed beyond recognition over the past thirty years and the ongoing process accelerated markedly following WTO accession. The underlying structure of the economy, however, remains remarkably unchanged. The state continues to own and operate about half the assets in the economy. State planning plays the major role in directing the allocation of resources. A state-owned banking system rations and allocates capital to help achieve politically determined goals. Furthermore, the distinction between the CPC and the state remains as blurred as ever. Despite the continued prominence of central planning, since engagement with the multilateral trading system, China has grown its exports to achieve the largest share in global trade since the US in 1968. About a quarter of global manufacturing now takes place in China. Macroeconomic policy, whether it is exchange rate management or overseas infrastructure investment, is geared towards ensuring market share gains in export markets. While China's economic success, as defined in a capitalist sense, has lifted hundreds of millions of people out of abject poverty, it has come at a massive cost too.

According to official statistics 240,000 Chinese workers died in over 1 million industrial accidents in 2002. This is a meaningfully higher annual rate of death than UK military casualties in World War I (885,000 over four years).[24] Although safety standards have improved, in 2015 there were still 66,000 deaths according to official statistics. Some would argue, and it would be hard to disagree, that such figures suggest a disregard for safety standards that we do not wish our liberal democracies to try to compete with. China's environmental degradation is notorious and, again, is evidence of the unlevel nature of competition in manufacturing trade.

Inequality of income and wealth have grown exponentially. A Gini coefficient measures inequality, where 0 represents perfect equality (everyone earns the same), and 1 perfect inequality, where all income is earned by just one person. In 2012, for example, according to the World Bank and a Peking University study, China's Gini coefficient was 0.49.[25] Among the most populous twenty-five countries in the world, only Brazil and South Africa had a more skewed income distribution. The paradox is that economies such as the UK and the US that are meaningfully more market driven have a *more* equal income distribution than centrally planned communist China. The sense of injustice this has generated has, arguably, more grounding than in the West because, rightly, much of this wealth accumulation is seen as being a function of corruption. Even in cases where the corruption is not criminal, the politicization of the economy means that economic success is intrinsically linked to Party membership or connections. Where the state controls resources, it largely determines the winners and losers. Connections (*'guanxi'*[26]) are perhaps the most important asset a businessman or woman in China can have. If one starts with the premise that for profit to be moral it must be made within the law (and the law is applied equally to all) and against fair competition, then a glance down the list of China's multibillionaires could leave one disappointed. The case of Evergrande, a property developer, is illustrative of the problem.

Few people outside China will have heard of the company called Evergrande, a property developer, or its major shareholder, Hui Ka Yan, who with more than USD40 billion of wealth has, on occasion, been China's richest person.[27] As of December 2007, Evergrande had just under USD3 billion of assets. By June 2017 total assets had risen to USD220 billion, funded by roughly USD24 billion of equity and USD196 billion of liabilities.[28] For context, if we exclude banks for obvious reasons, here are a few companies with assets similar to Evergrande: BMW, Walmart, Microsoft, Samsung Electronics, Total, General Motors and China Mobile (a state-owned Chinese telecommunications company). In fact, there are only about thirty companies in the world that are not banks or insurance companies with more than USD200 billion of assets. So Evergrande has grown from what most people would describe as a small company to a global giant in a decade by running up USD196 billion of liabilities largely to state-owned financial institutions. Microsoft, in contrast, took twenty-six years to go from USD3 billion in assets through the USD200 billion barrier. Now think what happened to the world of computing between 1993 and 2016 and Microsoft was at the forefront of it all.

Evergrande is by far and away the most leveraged and therefore most indebted company of its size in the world. What is more, its spectacular asset growth has been accompanied by persistent negative operating cash flow – in other words, there is nothing in the performance of the company that means the growth was generated organically.

What sort of incentive structure or what kind of financial thinking would lead an institution to extend credit to any company running such a balance sheet? The answer, surely, is nothing based on commercial considerations. What the rise of Evergrande and other 'private' companies illustrate, it could be argued, is how political control of finance can lead to favouritism and irrationality in lending practices: resources are allocated to the well-connected. The CPC monopolize not only political power but economic power too, and while the scale of Evergrande's indebtedness to state banks is unique, *guanxi* is omnipresent and a key part of China's economic system. No wonder those on the outside feel alienated and powerless to participate in anything other than a tangential way in the economic progress that China has made.

If inequality and a growing sense of injustice among its citizenry have accompanied China's economic rise in recent years, despite an indisputable rise in disposable income, how has liberal democracy in the West fared? The loss of manufacturing jobs has certainly accentuated geographical and social divides across Europe and the US. Of course, China's rise has not happened in isolation: other factors have been at work too. In Europe, the single European currency may well have contributed to the high level of unemployment in the more peripheral countries. Technology has undoubtedly contributed to some deflationary pressure on wages and supplanted employment in some industries, but the overriding change has been the introduction of a workforce of 750 million people (rising to about a billion) at rock-bottom prices into the global trading system.

As an increasing number of Chinese have been employed in export-orientated manufacturing, and their productivity has risen with infrastructure development and technology transfer, so the sense that they have won those jobs playing on an unlevel field has grown. What has also grown in the West is disillusionment with the 'free market' as a result of the unjust outcomes apparently delivered by engagement between the market economies of the West and the huge non-market economy of China. It can be argued, perhaps with some justification, that the election of Donald Trump or the decision by the British electorate to leave the EU and the rise of populist and extreme political parties in continental Europe are manifestations of just such disillusionment.

In the UK, the main opposition party is currently dominated by those who reject free-market economics entirely, and across Europe economic liberalism is in retreat. Across Europe populist parties are gaining ground and their most fertile soil is in the former industrial heartlands that have been hollowed out by globalization. If the hope of Western leaders was that economic engagement with China, through the WTO, would cement free-market economics and liberal democracy's hegemony in place for decades to come, it does not appear to be working out that way.

China's exporting prowess has been extraordinary, but to what extent can it be considered fair? The proponents of China's membership of the WTO consistently argued that the main benefit of tying China into the multilateral trade framework was to ensure that China played by the rules. Have they? Have those segments of Western society that have lost out because of economic engagement with China been on the receiving end of an injustice or did they receive their economic just deserts?

As China's trade surplus grew from its pre-WTO level of USD25 billion in 2001 to its 2008 level of USD300 billion, the argument about the underlying reasons for its gargantuan size raged. Among those that defend the surplus, the main argument has been that the surplus is due to a lack of savings in the West. The current account surplus (the degree to which exports of goods and services exceed imports) is identical to the degree to which an economy saves more than it invests. This is an algebraic identity, but it tells us nothing of the flow of causation or the transition mechanism that leads to it being true. In China, investment makes up a huge proportion of GDP (as high as 45%) and, since it runs a current account surplus, savings make up an even larger share. By contrast, in the US, investment was running at around 8% of GDP through much of the 1980s and 1990s but fell to the low single digits in the 2000s. The savings rate has been lower still, even turning negative in the late 2000s. The gap between what a country invests and what it saves has to be filled by foreign capital and since the balance of payments, by definition, balances, if a country has net inflow of capital it must run a current account deficit. Should a country not be able to attract capital to fund a current account deficit, the exchange rate would weaken to make both its assets more attractive to foreigners and its imports more expensive, thus remedying the situation, and vice versa.

With this in mind, imagine you are a consumer making a purchase in which you have a choice between an imported good from China and a domestically made alternative. All sorts of things might come into your mind for consideration, but I am certain that your thought process does not go along the following lines: 'I know Chinese people want to save a lot, more than they invest in fact, so knowing that they will be running a capital account deficit, I had better buy the Chinese good so that the balance of payments balances.' Consumers make choices based on price, quality and a range of other factors. The trade or current account surplus or deficit results from those choices. In a world in which capital for investment could not move across national borders, the exchange rate would move so as to adjust prices so that the current account was always zero. When capital *can* move across borders, a country can run a deficit on its trade account so long as a foreigner is prepared to fund that deficit. This is where the People's Bank of China (PBOC) comes into the equation.

As Chinese exporters met with huge success in selling goods, by offering products that people wanted at a price that they were willing to pay, they naturally wanted to repatriate their dollar revenues (most trade is denominated in dollars). Since China was exporting more than it was importing, there was a surplus of dollars being sold for renminbi. If a would-be seller of renminbi, did not emerge at the exchange rate that was prevailing, under market conditions the renminbi would appreciate until it reached a level at which there was a willing seller. The Chinese authorities, however, did not want the exchange rate to appreciate as this would damage their competitiveness in export markets. Instead, the PBOC would buy the dollars from the exporter with freshly minted renminbi. The dollars that the PBOC now owned, bought from a Chinese exporter through a bank, would be invested in US government debt and would become part of China's foreign exchange reserves, and the exchange rate would remain unchanged. The new renminbi created would expand China's money supply. The growth in China's foreign exchange reserves from USD170 billion in 2000 to USD3.8 trillion in 2014 is a pretty accurate guide to the extent of this intervention, or, as some would say, manipulation.

The exchange rate, therefore, between the US dollar and the renminbi was determined by the PBOC as a matter of national policy, designed to keep Chinese exports competitive, a policy in place since at least 1994. The purchasing power of the Chinese consumer in dollar terms was being suppressed by the exchange rate policy reinforcing the incentive to save, while the purchasing power of the Western consumer in renminbi terms was being enhanced, reinforcing the propensity to buy Chinese-made goods. Furthermore, by lending the dollar proceeds of intervention back to the US through purchases of debt by the PBOC, the American consumer could maintain a level of demand not justified by their now stagnating or even shrinking real incomes. Some have called this vendor-financing relationship symbiotic, but it was clearly unsustainable. From the perspective of the trade relationship though, what is clear is that the explicit exchange rate policy, which was in place before WTO accession and continued after it, was designed to help facilitate export success.

In a market-based economy, the decision to keep the notional exchange rate fixed would have ramifications. The increase in renminbi money supply – the direct consequence of buying dollars – would have (a) raised domestic demand, thus potentially sucking in imports to help equilibrate the current account, and/or (b) driven up domestic prices and costs. This rise in inflation would have led to a real exchange rate appreciation and eroded competitiveness. As is always the case, when you rig a market there are unintended consequences elsewhere. The growth in 'narrow' money caused by currency intervention formed bank reserves at the PBOC for China's banking system. The cash reserve ratio (CRR) determined the degree to which these could form the base for bank lending. If the CRR was 10%, each new renminbi at the PBOC allowed the bank to make RMB10 of new loans. If the CRR was 20%, then the bank could only make RMB5 of new loans. As foreign exchange reserves ballooned with China's current account surplus, the Chinese tried to limit 'broad' money supply growth (loans by banks) through increasing the CRR. This helped slow the potential rise in the domestic price level and thus elongated the duration of export competitiveness.

In the case of China, the expansion of money supply was done largely through state-owned banks and their lending was targeted at investment, bringing on new supply, rather than potentially import-intensive consumption. China could control the pace of urbanization and the supply of labour through the Hukou system, and so a key cost and determinant of competitiveness could be suppressed until the slack in China's labour market was exhausted. So long as state banks continued to lend to supply-enhancing infrastructure, connecting previously isolated cities with global markets, the key cost advantage of China – cheap labour – could be maintained. The fact that the banks were state owned meant that there was no need for the infrastructure projects to be cash generative or in any way 'economic' in their own right. They were to be viewed within the context of a national project. China's labour laws also helped keep wages and labour costs down in the face of the monetary expansion that resulted from currency intervention. Collective bargaining is banned in China and in the face of an apparently inexhaustible supply of labour, wages were slow to rise and lagged productivity growth in the early years of China's export explosion.

It isn't just the monetary architecture and the assets of the banking system that have been purloined for the national export project. Microeconomic policies have also been put to work: corporation tax reductions for export-orientated manufacturing; VAT rebates on exports; concessions on import duties for machinery used in the manufacture of exports; preferential lending terms from banks; and priority access to land have all been features of China's export drive. Many of these advantages were extended to foreign companies investing in China for export as well as to local firms and the result was the rapid growth in FDI. China made no secret of the fact that it wanted to attract export-orientated foreign investment, nor did it hide the fact that it wanted to be the beneficiary of technology transfer. As foreign companies built factories in China to export to the rest of the world, they brought with them machinery, technology and management know-how that could be copied and adopted to improve the efficiency of China's industrial complex.

Examples of China's abuse of intellectual property law range from the hilariously trivial to acts of national aggression. In between, of course, are thousands of examples of copyright breaches, brand bastardization, intellectual property theft and espionage that add up to a systematic, state-sponsored attempt to close the technology gap between China and the West. The advertising of 'Johnnie Worker Red Labial' 'Scotch' whisky is amusing, 'Crust' toothpaste is probably not as good as 'Crest' and 'Heimekem' lager may not be as refreshing as the real thing. Personally, I think 'Hike' is a better brand name for a sports shoe than 'Nike'. The remarkable similarity between the American F35 stealth jet fighter and the Chinese J-31 is more sobering and Western analysis of the J-31 suggests strongly that the performance gap between Chinese and American military hardware is closing fast as a result of espionage. In 2015, it was reported that when Segway, an American firm, accused

China's Ninebot, a specialist in transport robotics, of copying their two-wheeler product, the Chinese firm responded by buying out Segway to put an end to the lawsuit for patent infringement.

The overriding conclusion that can be drawn from the sixteen or so years of post-WTO economic engagement with China is that the Chinese economy has not converged on Western norms, as was hoped by many. China's success in manufacturing and exporting has come about due to market access combined with a mercantilist approach to economic management that is antithetical to Western norms. Furthermore, the clear injustice this has served upon large segments of Western society is not without political consequence.

If China's success in taking manufacturing and export market share were down to its natural comparative advantage, then the period of rapid growth in China's exports should have coincided with one of rapidly rising global productivity as economic resources were reallocated in a more efficient manner both in China and abroad. This has not been the case. Global productivity growth this century has been very disappointing despite some strong tail-winds from technological innovation. This fact tends to support the idea that China's success has been down to her mercantilist policies rather than any natural comparative advantage in the manufacturing of much of what she exports. Trade with China has led to the misallocation of scarce resources — the exact opposite of what free trade theory suggests should happen.

Chapter 4

China's Global Impact: Turning the World Upside Down

THE INCORPORATION OF CHINA INTO the global economy had the impact of changing relative prices across the globe with far-reaching effects. The real price of labour (wages adjusted for inflation) in the West fell, and this resulted in a corresponding rise in corporate profitability. The price of commodities rose sharply as Chinese incomes rose and their demand for resources that they did not themselves possess grew. This produced a boom in commodity-producing countries. The price of manufacturing goods fell as China was able to make them more cheaply. Household incomes in the West stagnated or fell in real terms while those in China and commodity-producing nations rose. The impact was to redistribute global income both between countries and within them. In some cases, this had been anticipated; in others not. Almost no country has been left unaffected by the changes.

At the turn of the century the global economy looked quite different from today. The 'core' of the world economy consisted of the US, the EU and Japan. Together these three economies (if one counts the EU as one economy) accounted for about 75% of global output and income. Collectively, the G3 as they are known was home to about 900 million people who enjoyed an income of about USD30,000 for every man, woman and child. Of course, there were other developed economies: Australia, Canada and New Zealand, for example, had similar living standards and a few developed European countries that were not in the EU should be included in arriving at the rule of thumb that about 20% of the world's population was responsible for 80% of its economic activity, enjoying per capita income in the region of USD30,000. In contrast, China itself accounted for another 20% of the world's population but only 3% of its economic activity. Income per person was less than USD1,000 a year or one-thirtieth of the developed world average. Manufacturing wages in even the most developed coastal Chinese cities were averaging in the region of USD1 per hour in 2000 in contrast to USD15 in the US.[29] Faced with this stark dichotomy it should have been apparent that the incomes of workers in the Western world were likely to come under severe downward pressure if or when they were brought into direct competition with their Chinese counterparts.

It is therefore not too surprising that the constituency that was most resistant to China's WTO accession in the West was organized labour. As a political lobby, trade unions were on the back foot. They had lost public support during the 1970s and 1980s through their belligerence and by fighting battles that were in the main against the broader public interest. Both their legal footing and their moral authority had been severely eroded in the run-up to China's accession. The riots in Seattle that accompanied the WTO meeting there exemplified the degree to which the anti-globalization movement was operating on the fringe of mainstream political dialogue. In short, by opposing virtually everything, no one was listening when they perhaps raised a valid point about China's entry into the global trading system. It was all too easy for corporate interests to portray their opponents as extremist fanatics opposed to any kind of market-orientated progress.

To be clear, not all labour was going to face direct competition from China. Many occupations cannot be carried out on the other side of the world. Administrative jobs in the civil service for example, service jobs in finance, teaching and healthcare, law enforcement and retail were immune, in the short run at least, from this change of gear in the process of globalization. Most vulnerable of all, of course, were those involved in manufacturing and particularly low-skilled, labour-intensive manufacturing. Anyone involved in the production of a good that was 'tradable' was at risk of seeing a very severe reduction in earning capacity or unemployment. As vulnerable, albeit maybe not so clear at the time, were the jobs of those that serviced the manufacturing communities: if one's customers lose their income, your livelihood disappears too.

Equally true, it needs to be stated, is that there were and are other low-cost production centres than China. The process of outsourcing or off-shoring production to lower-cost countries did not begin with China's accession to the WTO. China itself, as we have seen in the previous chapter, had been a meaningful recipient of FDI before 2001 and had been growing its exports off a low base. Indeed, other countries such as South Korea, Mexico, Thailand and Malaysia had for many years, stretching back to the early 1980s, pursued export-orientated development models where they sought to exploit their cheap labour to export to the developed world in much the same way that Japan had done in the 1960s through to the 1980s.

A number of factors, however, made China a special case. Ask anyone for a fact about China and they will most likely tell you that there are more than a billion people there, so the size of its population should not have come as a surprise to policymakers. In 2000 it was equally clear that the vast majority lived in what can only be described as abject poverty by Western standards. So, the wage differential between labour in China and the West should have come as no surprise. Yet these two facts alone – allowing 1.2 billion people and up to 750 million workers into a global trading system at a price of about 10% of the comparable 'first world' workforce

– should have set alarm bells ringing that this was not going to be an easy integration and that the consequences could be both dramatic and long lasting.

But the issues with China were more complicated than simply one of size and price. China had a long history of ignoring trade rules and abusing intellectual property rights. This was well documented and well known and was used perversely to argue in favour of their inclusion in the WTO on the grounds that exposure to WTO rules and a resolution mechanism would improve their behaviour. Change always brings with it winners and losers. While individuals or even whole segments of society that have lost out from China's integration might resent their new circumstances, wider society would be more willing to accept the outcome if economic justice is seen to have been served.

In the case of the economic victims of China's export push, this was not necessarily the case: the politicization of the economy in China meant they never stood a chance and their own elected representatives failed to protect their interests. China's export drive was a national mission and the apparatus of the state was put at the disposal of those who were a part of it. That entailed state-directed infrastructure investment, preferential tax treatment to encourage exports, state-allocated capital, manipulation of the labour market, direct and indirect input subsidies and clear manipulation of the exchange rate. While so-called market economies are quite capable of some of the above at times, it was and is the prevalence of *all* these factors in China that meant trade was being undertaken on an unequal footing.

Not all of China's gargantuan labour force could immediately be deployed in this big wage arbitrage opportunity. In 2000, only about 35% of the Chinese population lived in urban areas and could be easily put to work in export-orientated factories.[30] Infrastructure, although much improved over the preceding decade, was still substandard and therefore it was predominantly the urban workers in coastal cities that posed an immediate threat to Western labour. However, that amounted to a very meaningful workforce. Urbanization and migration towards booming export-orientated special economic zones meant that an additional 20 million mainly working-age Chinese were moving into cities each year. The bulk of population growth was taking place where the economic opportunities were to be had and so the supply curve of Chinese labour was far from fixed. With each passing year the incremental growth in the Chinese, coastal urban workforce was larger than the total manufacturing work force of the US, and every new rail and road link running away from the coast brought on new potential supply. This flexibility in labour supply – the ability of China through the Hukou system (the registration system that determines where a Chinese citizen is allowed to live) to increase the supply of labour by targeting urban migration – meant that as the capital stock in China rose and hence the productivity of labour increased, competition for jobs would help suppress wage costs relative to productivity gains. That is not to say wages did not rise; they did, but they rose slower than productivity gains.

Broadly speaking, there were two ways in which this new labour arbitrage opportunity could play out. Wage levels in the G3, adjusted for transportation costs and productivity, could drop rapidly and, as a consequence, the arbitrage opportunity would disappear and employment patterns in the G3 would be maintained but at the new, much lower price. Alternatively, jobs could be moved to the lowest-cost producer until the price of labour in China was bid up to a level at which the price gap disappeared.

The problems with the first scenario are all too apparent. Unions would not countenance such downward movements in wages; in many cases, minimum wage legislation forbade such cuts, and welfare payments as an alternative form of income would be a superior economic outcome to accepting Chinese wage rates as they then stood. Apart from anything else, it would be impossible to live in the

G3 on a Chinese wage, even adjusted for productivity differentials, at that time. The new equilibrium price for manufacturing labour in the developed world was incompatible with social stability. Given that a sharp downward move in wages was not going to happen in the G3, the alternative scenario of moving the jobs began.

Estimates of how dramatic the employment impact in the G3 of China's entry into the global trading system vary but, beyond doubt, in the sphere of manufacturing, where the competition for employment was most intense and direct, China had a dramatic effect on both the quantity and the price of labour in the G3. In the US, for example, five million manufacturing jobs were lost in the period 2001–2006. In both the US and the UK, manufacturing employment fell by roughly a third in the ten years following China's accession to the WTO. In the EU the percentage of workers employed in industry fell from 30% in 2000 to 25% in 2010 despite Germany's relatively successful trading relationship with China. In China itself, industrial employment actually rose as a percentage of total employment from about 22% to over 28%.

It was not just the loss of direct manufacturing employment though; the price of labour too came under severe downward pressure, and it should have been well understood that it would do so. Even in nominal terms, manufacturing wages in the US stagnated. Through the last thirty years of the twentieth century, median household income in the US grew at a steady pace of about 5.3%. In the first decade after China's accession to the WTO, that growth rate slowed to scarcely above 1% in nominal terms. In real terms the median household income actually fell 10% in that decade and even by 2016 had only just regained the levels of 2000. This phenomenon was not limited to America, of course. Wage growth in the UK has seen a similar absence, especially for those competing most directly with Chinese labour. In many of the more peripheral European economies, where manufacturing was of greater importance to overall GDP and where per capita incomes were lower and productivity levels more akin to those in China, the impact of China's entry into the WTO has been felt more acutely in the labour market. In such countries the impact of a massive supply shock, the availability of cheap labour outside the economy on an unprecedented scale, has been exacerbated by their inability to let their exchange rates adjust to ease the pain – by joining the single European currency, this was no longer an option.

Broadly speaking, as economic theory would suggest, the more flexible the labour market the less unemployment there has been as the price of labour has fallen in real terms, and this has borne more of the adjustment process than the quantity effect. But flexibility is not just about price. Where employers enjoy greatest freedom to hire and fire, job creation in new industries has been most rapid, so labour can be redeployed from areas where China has a cost advantage to areas that are not competing with China. This of course has meant that many well-meaning policies – such as minimum wage legislation and job protection laws – aimed at cushioning the lower-earning echelons of the population from the wage impact of China's integration with the global economy have exacerbated the problem not alleviated it.

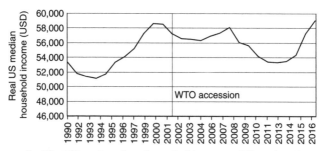

Figure 6. The US real median household income fell in the aftermath of China's trade success. *Source*: Bureau of Economic Analysis.

The inescapable conclusion is that economic engagement with China from 2001 onwards led to a rapid and dramatic deterioration in the real earnings power of workers in the developed world. There has not been a period in which median earnings in the developed world have been so stagnant for so long since the Victorian age. Over the same time frame (2001–16), however, nominal wages in dollar terms in China have risen about twelvefold. It was not just the developed world that was impacted though. Manufacturing workers in countries such as Mexico, Thailand and Malaysia have also seen their income stagnate or fall in real terms as the great labour arbitrage has run its course. Whatever the morality of the economic outcomes that have occurred since China joined the WTO, they have been far more dramatic than was admitted at the time. The suppression of the pricing power of labour, particularly manufacturing workers, has had and was always going to have far-reaching political consequences beyond the economic ones.

The labour arbitrage opportunity that presented itself offered companies the prospect of being able to produce goods much cheaper in China than in existing manufacturing centres. Under perfect competition these cost savings would be passed on to consumers in the form of lower prices and so theory would suggest that, as a result of China's entry into the WTO, China's exports would rise and the prices for these goods in developed markets would fall as the cost savings were passed on to consumers. If these cost savings were not passed on fully, corporate profit margins would rise, as costs were lower but prices remained the same. In other words, capital's share of the return (profits) would rise relative to labour's share (wages). Of course, it was also likely that the outcome would be a blend of both scenarios. As we discussed in the previous chapter (on China's economic transformation), China's exports did indeed grow: exponentially in fact. Their share of global exports rose at an unprecedented speed to a level not seen since America's domination of global trade half a century ago. But did this unlocking of China's low-cost advantage manifest itself in falling prices or rising profit margins or both?

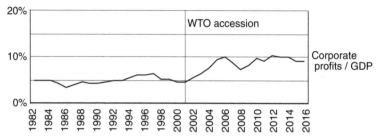

Figure 7. US corporate profits doubled as a percentage of GDP following Chinese accession to the WTO at the expense of wages. *Source*: Bureau of Economic Analysis.

The answer, perhaps unsurprisingly, appears to be both. Early academic work on the deflationary price impact of China's massive exports probably underestimated the impact. There are many reasons for this. Transfer pricing meant that the price that China did export at was not always the price it could export at. VAT rebates in China incentivized exporters to overstate the value of their exports. China started to move up the value chain and into new product markets making a continuous, meaningful and accurate time series of export prices difficult to construct. One of the clearly discernable but very hard to measure trends in Chinese manufacturing has been the steady improvement in quality. This is very hard to capture in inflation data but is obviously important. If the price of a good, say, a personal computer, remains the same but the quality, functionality and life expectancy all improve, then in real terms the price has actually fallen, but this may not be captured in the price data. In addition, as we will see, policymakers in the West fought this downward pressure on prices with easy monetary policy (low interest rates and the printing of money), so in some ways the correct measure of China's deflationary impact is not what actually happened to prices but rather what would have happened to prices in the absence of Western policymakers' intervention. Furthermore, there was a sense in which the mere threat of moving production to

China resulted in other countries curtailing price rises or reducing prices to remain competitive and avoid loss of market share. Competition with China led other producers to cut prices, including home base producers.

The indirect impact of manufacturing deflation, however, ran through many other additional channels. Lost manufacturing jobs, as a result of outsourcing, for example, created a pool of unemployed people who in turn suppressed wage demands for those workers operating outside the manufacturing sphere. Former factory workers were available to compete for service sector jobs. The ascent of China through the ranks of trading nations produced a policy response from other countries that fought back against their loss of market share. Japan, in its fight to maintain competitiveness, embarked on a systematic attempt to devalue the yen through monetary policy. The yen weakness of the mid 1990s was one of the catalysts, if not the root cause of, the Asian financial crisis. In the early years after China's WTO accession the issue of quantifying China's deflationary impact on the developed world was further confused by the bursting of the TMT (technology, media and telecoms) bubble in the West and, in particular, the US, and the recession that that brought about as investment shrank. This led Hu Angang, a professor of economics at Tsinghua University, to argue that it was a lack of demand in the G3 that resulted in the deflationary pressure of the early 2000s, not Chinese exports.[31] This was probably the consensus view at the time.

Hu's argument appears weak, although the policy response in the G3 implied, perversely, that he was correct. While Japan clearly was suffering from excess supply relative to demand, that was nothing new and had been the case for many years after the bursting of its own bubble economy in 1989. The US, though, never ran a current account surplus, or even came close in the 2000s – the last time was when it fleetingly brought its external account into balance during the recession of 1991. The recession of the early 2000s saw almost no improvement at all in the current account position of the US. The 4% of GDP current account deficit in March 2001 was a post-war record at the time. In other words, the US continued to consume more than it produced, to a record extent, even when its own economy shrank. As an aside, even the Great Recession of 2008/9 failed to move the US external accounts to balance.

The Eurozone, too, ran a current account deficit in 2000–2002 and any subsequent surpluses did not exceed 1% of its GDP until the height of the euro crisis in 2012 when domestic demand did indeed slide. The ramp-up in Chinese supply, coupled with its high savings rate, meant that China was producing more than it was consuming, hence the net exports. There was a lack of end demand relative to supply and it was in China not the West. Having run a current account surplus amounting to about 2% of GDP through 1998–2003, in the aftermath of China's WTO accession, the ramp-up of investment and hence supply, coupled with suppressed domestic demand (the flip side of a high savings rate), meant the surplus started to grow exponentially, reaching a staggering 10% of GDP in 2007Q3.

Writing in 2004 Steven Kamin, Mari Marazzi and John Schindler, who all worked at the Federal Reserve Bank, found strong evidence of the impact of Chinese trade on inflation but deemed the actual consequent depression of overall prices 'modest but not negligible'.[32] One of the issues they highlighted was that although Chinese imports were depressing import prices into the US, Chinese imports specifically and imports generally were a small part of the GDP of the US, and so the overall impact was in their view modest. In the run-up to the turn of the century, Chinese imports into the US were running at about USD8 billion per month. If they had written their research a few years later with data through to 2007, by which time imports from China were about three times more important relative to GDP, they might have reached a more damning conclusion. In any case, their analysis misses the point that competition from low-cost countries coupled with 'the law of one price' means that you do not necessarily need actual imports to reduce prices: the mere threat that they could come should keep prices low in the potential destination country in order to prevent an arbitrage opportunity arising. Prices are set at the margin. Furthermore, in the case of the impact on tradable goods and manufacturing, where China was competing, import penetration was many times higher.

If the suppression of wages in favour of corporate profits was one impact from China's entry into the WTO, a dramatic shift in the terms of trade between nations was another. China's comparative advantage, if you can call it that, lay in low labour costs and low regulatory standards. As global manufacturing growth was driven by China's new industrial complex, so this process produced winners and losers. As China's new-found wealth was deployed in housing and infrastructure investment, these different outcomes were exacerbated further.

Of all the countries that risked losing most from Chinese entry into the WTO, Mexico stood out. Indeed, for this very reason, Mexico was the last country to conclude bilateral trade negotiations with China before the latter's accession to the WTO. Mexico had become a member of NAFTA in 1994 and had been the recipient of large FDI inflows as a result. The 'Tequila crisis' had left the peso undervalued and multinationals were keen to exploit both the real effective exchange rate and the low labour costs that Mexico offered. Mexico, with uninhibited access to the US economy, was the perfect base from which to export to the US consumer. Through membership of NAFTA, Mexico had carved out for itself the perfect comparative advantage as a low-cost manufacturing centre for export to the US and Canada.

Mexico had enjoyed steady economic growth on the back of its liberal trading arrangement with its northern neighbours but China's accession to the WTO was to change that. Average monthly wages for manufacturing workers in Mexico in 2000 were about USD2 per hour; sixteen years later, they were still about USD2 per hour.[33] Total Mexican exports grew at a near 20% CAGR during the 1990s. From 2000 to 2007, that growth rate more than halved and from 2000 to 2017 the growth rate has averaged just 5%. Exports to the US underwent an even more marked slowdown from a growth rate of over 20% in the 1990s to a rate of just 5% almost immediately after Chinese entry into the WTO. With stagnating exports and wages it should be no surprise that Mexico's overall economic performance has been lackluster. From 1990 to 2001 the economy grew, in nominal dollar terms at 10%, more or less in line with China's own performance. Since then dollar-denominated nominal growth has averaged just 2.5% – scarcely higher than US inflation. This failure to move beyond middle income status despite its geographic proximity to and favourable economic ties with the global economic hegemon would have surprised observers back in 2001. One cannot but wonder if the current political friction between the US and its southern neighbour would be less intense if China had not 'eaten Mexico's lunch'.

If Mexico epitomizes what has happened to emerging economies, and indeed communities in developed economies too, that competed head-on with China in export-orientated manufacturing, then perhaps Australia epitomizes the winners from the world's attempt to integrate China. At the start of the century, few people would have forecast that Australia would grow three times as fast as Mexico, and yet that is what has happened. In the late 1990s and early 2000s Australian monthly exports to China were measured in the mere hundreds of millions of dollars. In fact, the first month in which they surpassed the USD1 billion mark was May 2005. They then rose eightfold in eight years through to the end of 2013, almost matching China's own export performance in the 2001–2007 period. This extraordinary boom was fuelled by China's demand for commodities, especially iron ore and coking coal for steel production and thermal coal for energy generation. In turn, this export performance drove the Australian dollar from being worth around 70c in 2005 to being worth over a US dollar, peaking at USD1.1/AUD in 2011. In consequence of the export boom and the currency strength, USD denominated GDP for Australia rose almost fourfold in the first thirteen years of this century.

While Mexico and Australia might represent the two extremes of how countries were impacted by China's exporting of manufacturing deflation and importing of commodity inflation, there were almost no parts of the world that were left unaffected by China's integration into the global trading system. As examples they serve to demonstrate how China's entry into the world economy resulted in a dramatic change to the terms of trade. The terms of trade of a country is the relative price of the things it exports relative to the price of the things it imports. China is importing huge amounts of commodities that it has insufficient quantities of at home. As a result, the price of these commodities rose – at least temporarily, until the supply could adjust accordingly. China was exporting manufactured goods from factories staffed by cheap labour, utilizing underpriced capital and operating under less stringent environmental and safety standards than elsewhere. Many of these factories enjoyed hidden or overt subsidies. Hence, the 2000s saw a rise in the price of the things that China needed and a relative fall in the price of the things that China produced. This in many ways reordered the global economic pecking order. In 2000, for example, the combined share of global income accounted for by the G3 (the US, Japan and the EU) amounted to about 75%; less than two decades later it was scarcely over half. In contrast, Brazil, through its oil and iron ore exports, has seen its relative importance rise. The hydrocarbon economies of Russia, the Caucasus and of course the Gulf have seen huge growth over the first part of the century relative to the erstwhile 'core'.

One of the more balanced outcomes is that of Germany. In 2000 German exports to China were running at about USD7 billion. By 2011 they had risen to about USD90 billion. In return Chinese exports to Germany had grown from USD15 billion to about USD90 billion over the same time frame. Total trade between the two countries grew spectacularly and the deficit all but disappeared. Almost uniquely, it has been a reasonably balanced relationship, with Germany exporting capital goods and importing lower-end manufactured products. Germany's share of Eurozone exports to China, however, rose dramatically from about 45% before WTO accession to over 55% by 2011, reflecting their success relative to their political partners in the Eurozone. By way of reference, Germany is about 25% of the Eurozone economy.

Germany's successful handling of China's integration into the global trading system was in part due to its membership of the single currency. Like China itself, Germany, or more precisely German exporters, has benefited from an undervalued currency. Monetary policy in the Eurozone is run for the benefit of the group of nations as a whole, and they enjoy very different productivity levels and growth rates. As Germany's productivity rose and as companies capitalized on the new global opportunities presented by trade, Germany's performance started to pull away from many of those economies that shared the euro. The relatively poor performance of economies such as France and Italy have helped keep the euro at a level that is too cheap to reflect the very successful German industrial machine. This has created a virtuous circle for export-orientated German companies, where success has not resulted in a dampening of its competitiveness through exchange rate appreciation as would normally have happened. Furthermore, immigration into Germany has helped alleviate the anticipated labour shortage, at least at the low end of the market. In some respects, euro membership has allowed the Germans to beat the Chinese at their own game, without the accompanying accusations of currency manipulation.

In the twelve months to the end of 2011, the Eurozone economies as a whole exported USD160 billion to China and imported USD305 billion from China, giving them a deficit of USD145 billion. They were importing nearly USD2 for every USD1 of exports. Exports, imports and the deficit had grown massively from the pre-WTO situation. In 1999 the deficit had been just USD24 billion and has therefore grown nearly sixfold. But, as is nearly always the case with the Eurozone, the aggregate or the average disguises a wide disparity of performance within the various disparate parts of this artificial economic construct. Taking Germany out of the equation, the situation was much worse than even the aggregate suggested. The starting deficit in 1999 was smaller at USD17 billion and because trade between China and Germany was more or less in balance by 2011, the entire Eurozone deficit was with countries other than Germany. The USD145 billion deficit, up eightfold in just over a decade, between China and the Eurozone minus Germany amounted to 1.5% of GDP.

The impact of China's internationalization, of its deliberate and well-executed pursuit of market share in world trade through mercantilist economic nationalism, was to have far-reaching consequences across the globe. Very few of these effects had been given any thought at all in the long debates that led up to the country's admission into the world trading community.

The two 'first-order effects', from which many others fructified, were the denigration of labour as a factor of production and the change in global terms of trade. The former led to more inequality within societies. The owners of capital were able to exploit the process of economic engagement with China to their advantage. Corporate profits as a percentage of GDP rose above a well-established fifty-year range and the rewards to owners of capital came through dividends, share buy-backs and capital gains. Those that relied on work for income saw their real purchasing power fall and in many cases, in the less flexible labour markets, spent time unemployed.

In contrast, the shift in the global terms of trade, at least ostensibly, may have helped reduce inequality between nations. Many poor but commodity-rich countries in Africa and elsewhere saw their growth prospects transformed. Whether these benefits accrued to the population at large is, of course, a different issue. Equally, however, the already rich Gulf prospered more and many developing countries that were dependent on manufacturing have gone backwards or stagnated in their development as a result of China's success.

The cost–benefit analysis of China's integration, from the perspective of the rest of the world, is further complicated by several issues, some of which are highly subjective but some not. From the standpoint of an economic liberal and a democrat, the commodity boom was a mixed blessing. For every Australia there is a Russia and for every Brazil there is a Mexico: some established democracies thrived, as did some authoritarian regimes. Some fledgling democracies benefited, and some, which needed nurturing and were politically aligned with the West, went backwards.

There are few industries that breed corruption more easily than the exploitation of natural resources. The commodity boom of the early 2000s was associated with a decline in governance standards at the national and corporate level, both of which have led to very real and direct economic loss. Furthermore, those developing countries that benefited from the boom may not continue to do so. The very nature of a commodity is that supply adjusts to the new demand and extraordinary profits evaporate as a result. The easy gains made by commodity rent seekers can cripple other parts of an economy. The hangover from the commodity boom that accompanied China's export growth and infrastructure building frenzy may undo many of the benefits that commodity-rich developing nations felt. The economic progress may be ephemeral but the potential political realignment, away from the West and towards China, may prove more permanent.

Within Western societies, too, the political reorientation, particularly of the young, is a cause for great concern, and the policy response to these first-order effects, as we will see, has exacerbated the problem.

Chapter 5

Making Things Worse: Inflation Targeting in an Age of Deflation

> If inflation is the genie, then deflation is the ogre that must be fought decisively.
> —Christine Lagarde

I T IS OFTEN THE CASE in the world of policymaking that one miscalculation leads to an even bigger mistake. Policymakers in the West clearly miscalculated the size of the impact of China's entry into the WTO. They severely underestimated the ability of communist China to capitalize on the new opportunity that was presented. They underestimated the impact this would have on the labour market in the developed world and the overall price level. The policy response of fighting the deflationary pressure with tax cuts, ever-lower interest rates and eventually the printing of money – all of which led to ever-more debt and inflating asset prices – exacerbated the social divides that globalization was already creating. The housing boom in the US of the early 2000s and the subsequent global financial crisis have, arguably, done more to discredit capitalism, its institutions and the market as a mechanism for allocating scarce resources than any other event since the 1930s. The ongoing ramifications pose a severe threat to the market economy and our free society. Perhaps some, or even all, of the above are understandable mistakes, or perhaps policymakers were too keen to indulge the vested interests for WTO membership in the first place. The dynamics that were unleashed by China's economic integration with the world were slow to be understood by many and, indeed, even now policymakers are hesitant to join the dots.

In January 2001, Bill Clinton left the White House and was replaced by George W. Bush. In the preceding three years, the US government had produced a budget surplus and was on course to do so that year as well. This was the first time the US government had been in financial surplus since 1969. The Chair of the Board of Governors of the Federal Reserve System, Alan Greenspan, was moved to air in public his concern that the Fed's ability to operate monetary policy might be severely compromised by the speed with which US government debt was going to be paid down. The surplus of 2000 was the largest relative to GDP since 1948. Throughout the late 1990s, the US economy had grown at about 4% per year, adding the equivalent of the size of the former Soviet Union's economy to its GDP each year. The US was on a roll. The White House was predicting a ten-year budget surplus in excess of USD1 trillion, but the early signs that things could be about to go wrong were already there.[34]

While the eventual productivity gains of the huge investment in information technology that took place in the late 1990s were real enough, the equity markets' perception of its monetary value was somewhat exaggerated. The easy monetary policy that was run in the aftermath of the Asian financial crisis and the subsequent Russian and Brazilian currency devaluations of 1998 and 1999 drove an asset bubble in TMT-related equities. Hence, after rising fivefold from the end of 1998 through to March 2000, the Nasdaq started to go into freefall. It was to fall 50% between March and the end of the year. The capital market bubble was bigger than the economic one, but nevertheless, there had been severe overinvestment in electronics and telecommunications in the late 1990s. Nine months after the bursting of the TMT financial bubble, the Fed started to respond to the slowdown in real economic activity. US and global economic growth slowed throughout 2001 and into 2002. In the end the recession was shallow (by some measures it was actually revised away as data were corrected) in comparison to those of the early 1980s and the early 1990s, but the threat of a very meaningful economic contraction was sufficient to produce an unprecedented monetary response from the Federal Reserve. Interest rates were cut 13 times between December 2000 and June 2003 to what was then a record low of 1% from a starting point of 6.5%.

As importantly, the new Bush administration passed two sets of tax cuts, one in 2001 and one in 2003. The economic slowdown obviously negatively impacted tax revenues, and the military conflicts that followed 9/11 added meaningfully to expenditure. Under this trifactor of influences, from a fiscal surplus of USD250 billion in 2000, the government's financial balance was in deficit to the tune of USD410 billion in 2003; relative to GDP this represented a five-percentage-point swing. What is remarkable, though, is that, despite the enormous fiscal easing and the then-unprecedented easiness of monetary policy, inflation remained very subdued and growth was slow to recover. Instead, debt increased, and the current account deficit ballooned. Greenspan need not have worried about the potential scarcity of government debt! While the Federal debt rose by just over USD1 trillion during the eight years of Clinton's administration, it rose by nearly USD5 trillion under Bush. Accommodative stabilization policy, both fiscal and monetary, was accompanied by a rising propensity of American households to consume and, in an increasingly globalized world, a rising tendency to import – particularly from China. America's current account deficit, which had been running at near record levels even as the US economy slowed in the early years of the century, grew to over 6% of GDP.

The problem with the deflationary pressure that China's integration caused was not just that it was unforeseen in its extent. Central banks had spent the preceding decades tackling inflation. Such was the bogey status of inflation that controlling it had become, in some cases, the sole aim of central banking. For others it was given equal importance with maintaining employment at close to a full level. 'Inflation targeting' as a policy had been put in place to prevent an uncontrolled rise in the overall price level: now it was to be deployed to prevent deflation. A successful stratagem for one war is not necessarily the best for the next one, and central bankers look increasingly like generals fighting the next war with the tactics of the last one, with disastrous consequences. At a time when technology was already having a dampening effect on the pricing power labour and companies could command, 750 million cheap workers were being brought into the global trading system. Furthermore, the same technological advances in telecoms and the internet were expanding the range of services that were becoming 'tradable' across borders and were therefore compounding the impact on wages and the labour market. In the absence of inflation, policymakers saw no need to constrain economic stimulus, even with the current account hitting new record deficits each year.

The purpose of the interest rate cuts was to try and stimulate domestic demand. The rationale was that the growth in output in the US was falling because there was insufficient demand. Yet going into the economic slowdown the US was consuming more than it was producing. Furthermore, this current account deficit was in place at a time when the government was running a fiscal surplus. In other words, it was entirely due to overspending by the private sector (households and companies) that the US was running this deficit and it was at a record level. A country that runs a current account deficit is, by definition, consuming more than it produces. The fact that on a net basis it is importing more than it exports means that, in addition to consuming its own output, it is also consuming a proportion of other countries' output. The disinflationary pressure that the US was experiencing in the early 2000s was not because of a lack of domestic demand – if that had been the case, the current account deficit would have narrowed dramatically and theoretically at least moved into surplus; it was because of a huge upward shift in the global supply curve caused by the introduction of those 750 million workers into the global trading system. For policymakers to influence aggregate demand relative to supply, they needed to either curtail Chinese supply or increase Chinese demand. The dearth of Chinese demand relative to supply, however, was in part a function of the structure of the Chinese economy and in part due to China's exchange rate policy. By keeping the renminbi undervalued, the Chinese were limiting demand for foreign-produced goods and services to the benefit of their exporters.

In November 2002, Ben Bernanke, who was to succeed Alan Greenspan as Chair of the Board of Governors of the Federal Reserve, made a speech entitled 'Deflation: make sure it doesn't happen here.'[35] In it he states:

> The sources of deflation are not a mystery. Deflation is in almost all cases a side effect of a collapse of aggregate demand – a drop in spending so severe that producers must cut prices on an ongoing basis in order to find buyers.

There is a footnote to the text of the speech, however, which reads:

> Conceivably, deflation could also be caused by a sudden, large expansion in aggregate supply arising, for example, from rapid gains in productivity and broadly declining costs. I don't know of any unambiguous example of a supply-side deflation, although China in recent years is a possible case. Note that a supply-side deflation would be associated with an economic boom rather than a recession.

In other words, if Greenspan and Bernanke had misdiagnosed the causes of disinflationary pressure in the US, the monetary response of cutting interest rates was going to be exactly the opposite of what was required. In late 2002, China was one year into its post-WTO accession export bonanza and academic economists using data from 1999 or 2000 had not yet picked up on the extraordinary rise in export penetration from China.

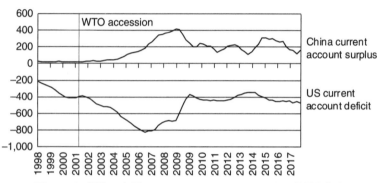

Figure 8. US and China current account positions (USD bn).
Source: World Bank open database.

The current account deficit that the US had been running in the late 1990s and into the early 2000s persisted through the recession of 2001/2 and then grew dramatically as demand rose further. When a country consumes more than it produces, it spends more than its income and the remainder is borrowed or financed by selling assets. The corollary of a current account deficit is rising indebtedness to outsiders: foreign capital is used to fund current purchases. The current account deficits were associated with rising levels of indebtedness, and an exceptionally easy monetary policy aimed at further stimulating domestic demand, by encouraging borrowing, added fuel to the fire. Since major investment in industrial capacity was not taking place in the US – while that was what was happening on a gargantuan scale in China – much of the domestic demand created by low interest rates went into either consuming imports or housing. The US economy moved relatively seamlessly from over-investment in TMT to overinvestment in housing.

Trying to stimulate domestic demand through interest rate cuts when the country was already running a deficit was probably the wrong thing to do. The US dollar weakened from 2002 through to 2007 as real interest rates were low or negative and the current account deficit was at record levels, but since the Chinese, with whom the deficit was widening most, had pegged their currency to the US dollar, dollar weakness against other currencies was insufficient to stop the deficit widening or correct the imbalance. Without Chinese exchange rate manipulation, the US dollar would have weakened against the renminbi and the current account positions of the two countries would have moved back towards balance.

The terms of Chinese accession to the WTO had not required them to stop intervening in the exchange rate. Chinese foreign exchange reserves rose from USD175 billion in 2000 to USD2.85 trillion in 2010. These reserves are the direct result of intervention in the exchange rate market to prevent the Chinese currency from appreciating. By preventing the natural adjustment in exchange rates from happening, the Chinese authorities were fuelling the debt build-up in the US. Equally, since the Americans knew what the Chinese were doing, policymakers in the US, by continuing to stimulate their own economy, should have realized that they were in effect going to stimulate Chinese growth. Not until resource utilization in China was exhausted and the labour arbitrage had run its course might inflation reappear. A prolonged period of negative real interest rates from the end of 2002 through to 2005 simply fuelled a speculative, debt-financed asset bubble in property. This bubble started to deflate in 2005 but it was not until 2007 that the full extent of the financial engineering and malfeasance that had taken place during this period of excessively easy monetary policy became obvious.

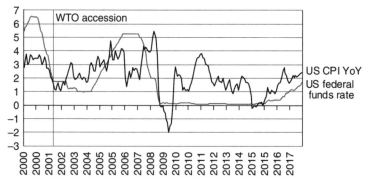

Figure 9. Real interest rates have been almost perennially negative to fight deflation. *Source*: Bureau of Economic Analysis and Federal Reserve.

So why were Greenspan and subsequently Bernanke and his fellow central bankers unprepared to tolerate deflation in the US and elsewhere? Inflation, and particularly unexpected inflation that is not priced into borrowing costs, represents a wealth transfer from people who save money to people who borrow money. The borrower will repay the principal using currency that in real terms is worth less than when he took out the loan. In addition, the interest rate, if fixed at a time of low inflation, may well be much lower in real terms over the course of the loan than was anticipated at the time the loan was made. Hence, inflation favours the indebted at the expense of the holders of that debt. As government has become bigger in the post-war period, so it has become more indebted. Governments borrow from both their own populations and sometimes from foreigners. Governments as debtors have a big incentive to keep inflation running in positive territory as this helps contain the real size of their indebtedness and hide the true degree to which they overspend relative to the revenue they receive. Governments, who after all control even supposedly independent central banks to a large extent, are a constituency that strongly favours modest but positive inflation.

The second constituency that strongly favours inflation or, more precisely, strongly opposes unanticipated deflation is the financial system. Banks take deposits and make loans. The repayment of a loan is much easier if inflation is continuously eroding the real value of the loan. Non-repayment, or default, if seen on a large enough scale jeopardizes the solvency of the banking system. Although there are circumstances in which deflation or disinflation can benefit banks, where say deposit rates (costs) fall faster than lending rates (revenue), a move to deflation or even genuine price stability is likely to make many loans unviable. The more leveraged the banking system is, the greater the jeopardy to the system from deflation and default. So the owners of banks (shareholders) are beneficiaries of modest inflation and potentially big losers from unanticipated deflation.

Not only do bankers support the low but steady and predictable inflation that makes the financial system of a leveraged economy (one in which various agents like government and companies have high levels of debt) more stable, it is also supported by the owners of assets who have used leverage to procure those assets – many borrowers! Companies who own assets see their profits inflated by borrowing as long as the returns on their assets are higher than their borrowing costs. Inflation means that these nominal returns will rise over time, and while the nominal value of their debt remains constant the companies appear to benefit too. Similarly, the reader will not need to have explained the benefits of owning a house (particularly a second one, which is a pure investment as opposed to a home) on credit when prices are rising (inflation). The leveraged impact on the equity component, the net worth of the asset after deducting the value of the debt, has been the most common method of wealth accumulation by households in the Western world for over thirty years now.

So, who loses out from this inflationary bias in monetary and fiscal policy? In general, as the overall price level rises, those without access to credit, those on a fixed income (pensioners) and those whose skillsets cannot command rising wages are the biggest losers, along with savers. Before the labour reforms of the 1980s, which saw the power of trade unions severely curbed, collective bargaining helped unskilled labour extract a higher rent than would have otherwise been the case. The combination of curtailed union activity and globalization means that nominal wage levels have come under severe downward pressure, particularly at the lower end of the labour market. The inflationary bias in monetary policy has resulted in a fall in real spending power for this segment of the population. Those on index-linked incomes such as the disabled and pensioners are in a better position because their incomes are linked to inflation, which in turn is meant to be an accurate reflection of their cost of living.

While lending agents (banks) and borrowers benefit from inflation, savers who hold cash and to some lesser extent savers who hold bank deposits suffer. Inflation erodes the real purchasing power of cash and in the current circumstance (and for much of the past twenty years) deposit rates have been insufficient to compensate for inflation.

Lastly, consumers generally benefit from falling prices. While some consumers may postpone purchasing decisions in a deflationary environment to wait for things to get cheaper, most people buy what they want when they need it, without waiting. Deflation should be the normal course of things. As a society becomes more efficient at producing goods, so prices should fall – it is only money illusion that stops this from happening. In real terms (say, measured in the number of hours required to buy something), things should and normally do get cheaper. By preventing prices in aggregate from falling, central banks have tended to penalize consumers to the benefit of producers.

As interest rates were cut dramatically in the early 2000s and as central banks have been forced to adopt more and more extreme policies to prevent deflation and hit their self-imposed inflation targets, they have been keen to portray their policies as not only necessary but, importantly, as apolitical. The cult of the central bank has grown up around the idea that monetary policy is politically neutral and should therefore be carried out by technocratic experts, free from the constraints of the political cycle. This argument seemed very persuasive when the key battle that central banks were fighting was to rein in runaway inflation, which was thought to require the politically awkward imposition of a period of unemployment. This was a responsibility that elected politicians were keen to distance themselves from. Since the early 1990s, the public's expectations of central banks have risen and expanded. The sense that central banks are omnipotent – that they can prevent recessions, elevate asset prices, produce full employment and control inflation all at the same time – has become common currency. Recessions, rather than being seen as an unpleasant but important part of the economic cycle, rather as winter is an unproductive but crucial part of the seasonal cycle, became viewed as an unnecessary consequence of policy failure. Far from producing long-sighted, visionary policymaking, the veneer of central bank independence has subjected central bankers to the same pressure from public opinion as their political masters and resulted in the same tendency towards expediency but without democratic legitimacy. Yet the wider the range of things that it is claimed central banks can achieve, the greater the chances of failure.

By clearly understanding who has won and who has lost from the inflation bias in monetary policy, it is evident that the policy is anything but apolitical. The cost of acquiring an old-age income through savings during your working life has risen exponentially as financial asset prices have been driven up first by low interest rates and then by quantitative easing (QE). The higher the asset price at any point in time, the lower the future return will be on that asset. This has a very real impact on wealth distribution along the lines of age. Those who were old enough to have made meaningful contributions to their pension schemes before QE have benefited from the asset price inflation; those who were too young will start to save for old age by buying inflated, low-returning financial assets from their parents' generation. An old-age pension is perhaps one of the two most expensive purchases most of us make during the course of our lives, but few of us realize it.

The most expensive purchase that many of us make, on average, is housing. This is true whether we buy or rent. There are very few, if any, advocates of QE or inflation-biased monetary policy who would not accept that the policies they have advocated have had a big impact on housing costs in the Western world. In recent years, the rising cost of housing, coupled with stagnant incomes, has made property ownership an unattainable goal for millions of younger people entering the workforce. This is tremendously dangerous in many ways. The popular appeal of capitalism in the 1980s and beyond depended on its inclusiveness, and the widest possible ownership of property was a key ingredient of the democratic success of the exponents of capitalism. Extolling the virtues of home ownership is hollow if a large and growing segment of your electorate can no longer afford to buy even the most modest of homes.

Targeting a rise in the overall price level of say 2% per year, as many Western central banks do, when the 'tradable' portion of the basket has been falling in price, has inevitably led to higher levels of inflation for the 'non-tradable' part of the consumer basket. The main benefit of globalization for the Western consumer was supposed to be a lower cost of living as cheap imports from the developing economies were made available. That benefit, however, has been deliberately removed by a policy of inflating the price level of the non-tradable products that go into making up the total cost of living. Meanwhile, the increased level of wage competition from the huge increase in the supply of labour has squashed wage inflation in the developed world to the benefit of corporate profits. The consequence of the easy monetary policy required to meet the inflation target, or at least the attempt to, has produced asset price inflation and a level of leverage (financial borrowing) in the economy that makes a change of policy direction without a debt crisis almost an impossibility. As a result, the West has found itself stuck in a vicious cycle of ever-increasing indebtedness, low household income growth but rising asset prices as a by-product of central bank insistence that the overall price level keep rising. Imprudence has been rewarded while thrift has been penalized, and increasingly the institutions of capitalism have been discredited in the eyes of the electorate.

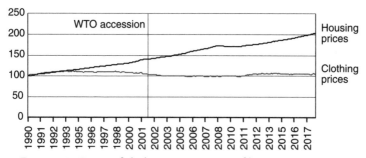

Figure 10. Prices of clothing versus prices of housing 1990–2017.
Source: Bureau of Economic Analysis.

Clearly, the blame for the global financial crisis that hit the world economy in 2008/9 cannot be placed wholly on communist China, although the deflationary forces that economic engagement with China unleashed were a necessary but not sufficient ingredient in the mix. The prime cause of the crisis was the confluence of those deflationary forces with the Western central banks' policy of inflation targeting and their determination to prevent deflation. This in turn was dictated by the indebtedness of our governments and the leverage that had been built into Western financial systems as a result of thirty years of inflation bias in monetary policy. Iron-ically, many of the same institutions that were in the vanguard of lobbying in favour of China's entry into the WTO – multi-national companies such as General Electric and financial com-panies such as AIG – also embraced the inflation bias in monetary policy, and, after leveraging themselves up, fell victim to the crisis of 2008 when the bubble burst. In other words, they were hoist by their own petard. It was the easy monetary policy of the preced-ing decades, and the behaviour that that encouraged, meeting the deflation from China that created the backdrop to the crisis. These factors resulted in the environment in which all the varied short-comings of regulation, conflicts of interest and sheer greed could combine to bring about economic and financial catastrophe and discredit the market economy in the eyes of so many. The potential rise in the esteem with which a neutral observer might view China's economic system, judging it by the results of the 2000s, was now complemented by the obvious failings of the Western economic system created in the era of globalization.

Chapter 6

Hearts, Minds and Wallets: Washington versus Beijing

China is marking a path for other nations around the world who are trying to figure out not simply how to develop their countries, but also how to fit into the international order in a way that allows them to be truly independent.

— Joshua Cooper Ramo[36]

FROM THE EARLY DAYS OF post-war globalization and trade, some of the actions of Western policymakers have alienated lesser-developed countries. Allegiance to the existing global economic order was driven as much by the lack of a credible alternative as anything else. The economic rise of China has the potential therefore to lead to a dramatic realignment of loyalties unless the existing order is seen to be more egalitarian in its treatment of developing nations. The events of the twenty years running up to China's accession to the WTO created a fertile ground for China in its attempt to spread its economic hegemony throughout the region.

In August 1979 Paul Volker became Chair of the Board of Governors of the Federal Reserve System, a role he was to remain in for eight years. The money printing that was required to finance America's military involvement in Vietnam coupled with the oil price shocks of the 1970s had produced a period of runaway inflation and Volker's mission was to put an end to it. In early 1980 US inflation was flirting with 15% and the Fed raised rates aggressively to a peak of 20% in 1981. The bitter medicine worked insofar as inflation fell precipitously but at the cost of a deep, double-dip recession and high unemployment.

Domestically, Volker's policy was and still is widely regarded as a necessary one that paved the way for the rapid economic expansion of the 1980s and 1990s, which in turn raised American living standards dramatically, although the policy is not without its critics. Internationally, however, there were very significant ramifications. The abandonment of the gold standard in the 1970s had meant that the US dollar had become the de facto global reserve currency. Almost all trade was denominated in dollars and so countries wishing to purchase imported goods had to keep a prudently sized stock of dollars to pay for them. The dollar, being freely exchangeable and with the backing of the world economic and military hegemon, became nearly universally acceptable as a medium of exchange and often substituted for local currencies where the monetary authorities were prone to abuse their power. Developing countries, particularly those in Latin America, had borrowed heavily in dollars to finance their industrialization policies, in part from the Middle Eastern countries that had benefited so much from the high oil prices of the 1970s. High US interest rates, instigated by Paul Volker in his inflation battle, made those borrowings expensive and ultimately unaffordable and, inevitably, defaults followed. The resulting economic malaise cost the continent dearly in terms of lost output and a reversal of much of the social and economic development that had been made in the preceding period. One of the lessons that should have been learnt from the whole debacle was that US monetary policy, now that the dollar was the global reserve currency, had international ramifications of potentially enormous economic and geopolitical significance. The Latin American debt crisis of the early 1980s was the first of a string of emerging market crises that were triggered, if not caused, by American monetary policy.

The advantage that accrued to the US economy by having the US dollar as the global reserve currency came with responsibilities that, if ignored, had the potential to put a shelf life on the dollar standard. What was missing was a credible alternative. Soviet rivalry provided an incentive for America and her allies to woo the developing world. The surest way to procure and keep allies was to demonstrate that the adoption of your values produced higher living standards and social progress. The recession of the 1980s, the Latin American debt crisis and the ensuing lost decade demonstrated the dangers that domestic economic policy could pose to America's international standing.[37]

As things turned out, the collapse of the Soviet Union and the apparent failure of economic planning as an economic model, both in Russia and its acolyte states, served as something of a temporary panacea for latent resentment of the apparent American indifference to the international ramifications of domestic monetary policy. There was simply no alternative. The widening acceptance of large parts of the free-market economic model among developing countries during the 1990s, however, should not be confused with an ideological commitment to broader Western values.

The US recession of the early 1990s that followed from the savings and loan crisis produced a period of easy US dollar monetary policy. The ensuing low interest rates and weak US dollar resulted in rapid capital flows towards emerging markets and in particular Asia. As the US economy recovered in the mid 1990s and as US interest rates normalized, the dollar started to gain in value. Asian countries that had pegged the value of their currencies to the dollar started to see monetary condition tighten in lock-step with what was happening in America. There were, of course, many underlying fault lines in the economies of Asia that made them vulnerable to policy swings elsewhere, but in the recriminations that followed the collapse of many Asian economies and the exchange rate devaluations of 1997 and 1998, the internationalization of the dollar, foreign investors and the institutions that oversaw the dollar standard made easy targets. The policy prescriptions of the IMF and the World Bank, fiscal austerity and tight monetary policy stood in stark contrast to the policies that had been pursued in the West during times of economic hardship. The apparent hypocrisy was jarring.

China, on the other hand, by not devaluing the yuan in the late 1990s, managed to portray itself as a stalwart friend of the suffering countries in its hinterland. China, in fact, continued to run current account surpluses throughout the Asian crisis without devaluation: a currency adjustment was not needed as the yuan was chronically undervalued following its own previous devaluation of 1994. The devaluation of 1994 itself should have served as a warning of China's mercantilist intentions and in fact had contributed to the Asian crisis as China started to take market share in exports at the expense of its neighbours. Nevertheless, the kudos China earned was to stand it in good stead in its negotiations for WTO accession and its future dealings with ASEAN and its other Asian neighbours. Its behaviour was to be cited as evidence of the country's maturity and benevolence towards the region and China was able to emerge from the aftermath of the Asian crisis with its image as a responsible and benign player on the international stage much enhanced.

America's increasing military belligerence, the perceived hypocrisy in the treatment of the developing world in the Uruguay round of trade talks, and the intrusive nature of the policy prescriptions following the various financial crises in emerging markets were contributing to the impression that supposedly multilateral organizations were acting almost exclusively in America and the West's interests. Against this background, China's economic rise in the first decade of the new millennium could be seen as something of a triumph for those looking for an alternative to the unipolar world that the demise of the Soviet Union had produced.

If the aftermath of the emerging markets crisis of 1997–99 set in place some of the conditions for a realignment of political allegiances away from Washington and towards Beijing, the subsequent financial crisis a decade later reinforced and accelerated the trend. The Enron scandal and the bankruptcy of WorldCom showed that conflicts of interest and institutional shortcomings were not confined to the developing world. The housing bubble and its bursting called into question the prescience of the Federal Reserve and the quasi-governmental lending institutions. The credit rating agencies were discredited, if you'll excuse the pun. Bank nationalizations and bailouts at the taxpayers' expense and the fiscal deficits that these required were in stark contrast to the principles that the liberal Western policymakers had advocated emerging countries follow at times of economic crisis. Having preached against fixed exchange rates, the euro project seemed to be emulating the policies that the international monetary authorities had ridiculed. When the euro crisis erupted in 2010–11, the resources of the IMF were purloined in a fashion and in a size that seemed almost designed to alienate long-suffering developing nations for whom the rules had not been bent. In short, the interaction between governments, central banks and the institutions that dominated the commanding heights of the market economy in the West in the period from 2000 to 2009 could not have been better designed to undermine the moral standing of the capitalist model if one had set out to do so.

However, having seen how the West became its own worst enemy, are there any lessons other countries should take from China's rapid economic progress, or is this a case of Chinese exceptionalism? Just how culpable are American or Western policymakers in fostering an international backlash against the then-existent world order? Furthermore, does China represent a benign alternative to

American hegemony or are third countries simply swapping a system stacked in America's favour for submission to the interests of the CPC?

Perhaps the most legitimate and long-standing of the complaints against the US-dominated organizations that have overseen the global economy in recent decades, from the perspective of third countries, revolve around Western protection of its agricultural industry to the detriment of developing nations. There has been an asymmetry in the level of openness that has been negotiated for manufacturing and even services, relative to agriculture, which certainly supports the argument that emerging economies are being denied fair access to developed-world consumers for their agricultural produce. The hypocrisy that this has entailed has been a legitimate and long-standing source of resentment among developing nations.

Western-led policy in response to emerging market debt crises has also attracted criticism. There has certainly been a degree to which policy has been intrusive and even compromised some notions of national sovereignty, although it would be hard to argue that in modern times multilateral institutions have behaved more aggressively than past hegemons in defending the rights of creditors. Britain, after all, invaded Egypt partly to protect its economic interests, and Newfoundland famously was forced to surrender its sovereignty entirely as a result of a financial crisis. That aside, much of the advice and suggested reforms have, at least up to a point, been well intended and generally successful. They have, however, trodden on the toes of vested interests and evoked criticism from these parties. Breaking the nexus between politicians, banks and industrial holding companies was never going to be popular among the owners of such corporate empires or their acolytes in politics. A review of the behaviour of Western governments in the aftermath of the 2008 crisis, however, would suggest that a similar nexus has been created in the West and the policy response has been diametrically opposite to that prescribed by the IMF to less-developed countries.

As for monetary policy, the vagaries of which have produced a 'feast or famine' impact on emerging economies for much of the past forty years, it is hard to see what the Federal Reserve could have done differently. Their mandate is a domestic one, and the US is a big and varied enough country to make a single interest rate a cumbersome tool for managing output and the price level. There is a case for saying that the Fed should have paid more attention to the consequences of their actions in a broader variety of variables, such as debt accumulation and domestic asset prices, a sudden change in which might impede their ability to meet their stated targets. To extend this to saying that they should be running monetary policy with an eye (or even half an eye) on the implications for other countries is a big leap and would be asking the impossible in a practical sense.

The Americans, as a point of policy, have encouraged the use of the dollar in global trade, but others have voluntarily agreed to it. If, say, the Europeans and Saudi Arabians wish to trade oil in euros, there is nothing to stop them. More often than not, it has been the repeated abuse of power over fiat money by others (debasement through wanton printing) that has led institutions and countries to turn to the dollar. That is why the monetary policy in the US during the Greenspan, Bernanke and Yellen years should perhaps have led to a challenge to the dollar standard, if only there was an alternative. In short, the dollar standard is voluntary, and the Fed's mandate was clearly defined. Those who peg their currencies to the dollar know they will be inheriting a monetary policy designed to meet US domestic goals, and they sacrifice domestic economic stability in return for the hope of exchange rate stability.

More recently, under the leadership of Dominic Straus-Kahn and then Christine Lagarde, the IMF, through its dealings with the Eurozone, has fuelled the anger of the developing world. The

Fund's resources were effectively purloined to rescue a politically inspired project, the single European currency, that made questionable economic sense. Economic forecasts were doctored to fit the political agenda and there was little doubt that Greece would have to undergo a debt restructuring anyway. The IMF's rules prohibit it making loans to countries that cannot pay them back, as was clearly the case for Greece. Quite rightly perhaps, the abuse of the IMF for the furthering of the 'European Project' has lent meaningful credence to the argument that the IMF is not fit for purpose. The result has been the formation of the Asian Infrastructure Investment Bank (AIIB) under China's leadership: a clear example of a misstep by the West presenting an opportunity for China.

While Western-dominated international economic institutions may well have lost some support from developing countries through their inconsistent behaviour, in terms of China's economic influence on third countries, there are really two questions. Firstly, to what extent is China's economic development model replicable insofar as it differs from the prescriptions of American neoliberalism? And, secondly, to what extent can China be an alternative source of investment, trade and financial assistance to help developing countries make economic and social progress and at what cost to their independence?

In 2017, China's per capita GDP, according to the IMF and adjusting the nominal number for purchasing power parity was USD16,624, making it 96th out of 187 countries. Using nominal numbers, but no PPP adjustment, per capita GDP of USD8,600 put China 72nd. While the rankings put China above the median, mean world per capita GDP is over USD10,000, and so despite forty years of economic reform and rapid progress China's economic outcome in this regard remains disappointing. Furthermore, China's sheer scale is matched only by India. Many other populous developing economies – for example, Brazil, Mexico, Russia and Turkey – remain better off than China, although their recent growth rates have been more subdued. One of the factors that has been responsible for China's successful growth has been its demographics, the control of which is largely beyond the scope of policymakers. China's working-age population grew more than 50% from below 600 million in 1980 to 950 million in 2010, and while that is partly taken account of in the per capita calculation, what is not captured is that the proportion of the population of working age as a percentage of the total population grew from about 60% to roughly 75% over that period. With three potential workers for every non-working-age person, rather than one and half when reform started, the scope for rising per capita income is obvious. This demographic dividend is now spent and from now on this will work against economic growth in China. So, not only is per capita income in China not actually that enviable on a global comparison, the China model has benefited from a one-off demographic boon that other policymakers would not be able to replicate.

China's scale had two other important ramifications for growth. The eagerness of foreign companies for access to the domestic market resulted, as we have seen, in a strong, privileged diplomatic negotiating position that is not enjoyed by many developing countries. If it is the case that China managed to combine a dictatorial nationalistic economic policy with access to developed world markets by leveraging the self-interest of multinationals, it is far from obvious that such a strategy would be available to other emerging economies.

China's scale also manifested itself in it being the preeminent destination for FDI complete with meaningful technology transfer. China's high savings rate, which allowed for a high rate of investment without incurring foreign indebtedness, was certainly a major driver of productivity and therefore economic growth. To the extent that high savings were driven by a policy of undervaluing the exchange rate, it came at a cost in terms of the misallocation of resources and to the extent that high savings were a function of unique cultural factors, it is by definition not replicable elsewhere. Inculcating a higher propensity to save and invest is by no means impossible but replicating China's national experience is probably not an option. China was able to mobilize the high savings through a state-owned banking system by ensuring that there were few if any credible alternative destinations for these savings. Banks were able to offer low, sometimes negative, real returns on those savings. While the savings monopoly enabled the Communist Party to allocate capital to its chosen recipients, it is far from clear that this aspect of China's development model was a contributor to its success rather than a hindrance.

Disaggregating the contributing factors to China's supposed economic success does not throw up many unique and replicable attributes that differentiate the Chinese model from those pursued by other emerging economies. There have been plenty of one-party states that have failed to develop fast. State-owned banking systems practicing financial repression have more often than not squandered a nation's resources. The lack of political opposition, the use of coercion to control (through the Houkou system) the rate of urbanization, and the state monopoly of the media have all contributed to giving the impression of a unity of purpose and lent a nationalistic bent to the process of economic development but whether they have actually added to productivity is highly debatable. The ability of the state to requisition land for property development or for infrastructure projects with minimal consideration for the previous occupants has certainly helped expedite development at a speed that would be the envy of, say, India. Similarly, disregard for worker safety and environmental protection has helped lower costs and speed up development, but this is not a development model most other countries will want to emulate.

While China has added somewhere between USD14,000 and USD8,000 to its per capita GDP since 1980, depending on how it's measured, the US has added USD40,000 and the UK USD30,000 to their per capita GDPs, a result so significantly superior as to circumvent any debate about the nuances of measurement. Japan, often thought of as the poster child of economic disaster in recent decades, has added USD30,000 to its per capita GDP since 1980. Nor has China just underperformed – by this perhaps most relevant measure – those countries that had already 'made it'. South Korea has seen its per capita GDP rise from less than USD2,000 to almost USD30,000, adding USD25,000 per capita, three times China's improvement. The data all seem to point to the inescapable conclusion that the rapid growth rate in China's economy is almost exclusively down to the low starting point rather than the discovery of an economic elixir. Furthermore, such growth as there has been was the result of the limited adoption of elements of the Western system, combined with access to export markets and high domestic savings. Some of the Chinese characteristics may well have had a detrimental impact.

Equally, it is important to recognize that there are many developing economies that have not been able to capitalize on the global economic infrastructure in place over the past forty years. The ability of the US to run perennial current account deficits, to borrow from abroad in its own currency, to buy from abroad using freshly minted dollars, and to maintain an independent monetary policy to cushion its economy from the vagaries of the economic cycle – all has been cause for resentment. In short, the dollar standard – the monetary architecture in place since the 1970s – has worked in America's interest. Add to that the hypocrisy of agricultural protectionism and the overly prescriptive policies of the Washington consensus as espoused by the IMF and the World Bank, and what has resulted is fertile territory for a China looking to expand its global influence.

While China's economic model may not be producing superior results per unit of input, the sheer scale of the country means that a suboptimal outcome per person still adds up to a powerful economy. This is very different from the old Soviet–US rivalry, where competing economic models were being tested on a similar scale. An inferior Chinese economic model could well produce an economy larger than America's. It could certainly, and may be about to, become more relevant to a large portion of the developing world.

In late 2013, Xi Jinping unveiled China's Belt and Road Initiative (BRI). At one level BRI is a giant infrastructure project, or perhaps more precisely a series of infrastructure projects. The aim is to promote cross-border trade and investment among the sixty or so countries that the initiative is slated to impact. To this end, the Chinese are constructing roads, railways, bridges, dams and power plants to open up and connect markets.

There is undoubtedly a genuine need for an increased level of infrastructure investment in the region and to that extent it is hard to do anything other than endorse the plan. The construction process will provide a market for China's building materials industry that suffers from, in some cases chronic, overcapacity.

The trade and investment associated with the plan will also help achieve another of Beijing's stated objectives: the internationalization of the renminbi. It is hoped that trade and investment between China and the nations who receive Chinese largesse will be denominated in renminbi. In doing so, the aim is to create a renminbi bloc, a trade region in which the renminbi gains credibility both as a means of exchange and a store of value, displacing the role of the US dollar. If there is to be a transfer of benefit from the US to another power from a transition to a multicurrency reserve system, China wants to be at the front of the queue for such a dividend. China's financial largesse will also likely come at a price in terms of support and influence. In fact, it is unclear to what extent China will finance these projects. How much will be given as opposed to lent, and on what terms? What proportion of the work will be carried out by Chinese companies? Will they be state owned or private? What sort of margins will they make? It is quite possible that what BRI boils down to at an economic level is state-backed vendor financing, piggy-backing off China's sovereign rating.

It appears that such a vast undertaking requires its own institutional infrastructure and to that end the AIIB has been set up with USD100 billion of authorized capital and the USD40 billion Silk Road Fund will invest in companies operating along the various infrastructure corridors. These financial institutions rival Western-dominated ones based in Washington: the IMF, the World Bank and its subsidiary, the International Finance Corporation (IFC). The establishment of these institutions somewhat lifts the veil on what are perhaps China's real intentions with this undertaking: a geopolitical land-grab.

China's rise to preeminence as the factory of the world has brought her into contact with many countries that supply the raw materials for her new industrial complex. China's thirst for hydrocarbons has reshaped her relationship with Russia and the Caucasus. Her demand for coal and iron ore has led to greater economic engagement with Mongolia (more than 80% of Mongolian exports go to China). In Africa, China has risen in importance as a destination for the continent's raw material exports and is now the dominant trading partner for many countries.

At the same time as the West has retreated from manufacturing, so its importance as a trading partner for these suppliers of raw materials has diminished, leaving a void of influence. As China's demand for raw materials has increased and, as a consequence, new trading relationships have developed, new markets have been found for her exports too. About a third of imports into Pakistan, Kyrgyzstan and Myanmar, for example, come from China. These trading relationships are what has motivated the BRI: opening markets for exports and securing supply lines of raw material imports.

In the same way as China's manufacturing dominance makes her the main destination for trade for many countries in Eurasia and Africa, BRI, it is hoped, will make her the main source of overseas investment and that will bring with it political influence.

The reorientation of political allegiances among developing countries towards China is a function of China's importance as both a trading partner and as a potential source of development capital, which has stemmed directly from China's success in dominating global manufacturing. This in turn has, to a large degree, depended on the unfettered access to Western markets that WTO accession bestowed.

At the time of writing, this reorientation amounts to only a modest degree of rivalry between China and the West for the political allegiance of third countries. One factor that could accelerate the loss of American, and more broadly liberal democratic, hegemony would be the collapse of the dollar standard and its replacement by a rival monetary order. That is why the internationalization of the renminbi is a key objective of the BRI.

Under a system where the dollar was the sole reserve currency, and nearly all trade was denominated in dollars, countries were incentivized to store dollars (foreign exchange reserves) to finance future import needs. These were earned by running trade or capital account surpluses. The IMF advised that countries have reserves equivalent to at least three months' worth of imports. By holding these reserves (usually in the form of US government bonds), they were effectively lending back to the US the money they had earned by selling them goods and services. Like Japan before it, and in conjunction with other Asian countries that pegged their exchange rates to the dollar, however, China accumulated foreign exchange reserves far in excess of what was required for precautionary reasons. These huge reserves were a function of intervention in the foreign exchange market to prevent their currencies from appreciating against the US dollar. In the past decade or so, managers of these national reserves have made an effort to diversify away from dollars to other currencies to produce a basket of reserves aligned to the country of origin of their imports. But since most trade, in particular in oil and commodities, remains dollar denominated, the US currency has maintained an outsized weighting in foreign exchange reserves.

Between 1990 and 2010 China's foreign exchange reserves rose from a few billion dollars to nearly USD3 trillion. Since China did not want the renminbi to appreciate against the dollar, so that it maintained its cost competitiveness, the PBOC, the central bank of China, purchased the dollars earned by Chinese exporters with freshly minted renminbi. In this way, the amount of renminbi in circulation became directly linked to the size of China's balance-of-payments surpluses. The huge surpluses that followed WTO accession produced massive growth in China's money supply, bringing interest rates down and encouraging bank lending, which in turn increased the money supply further. Hence, the expansion of debt in China and with it rising property prices and investment in capacity and infrastructure were direct consequences of the trade and capital account surpluses China was running. Because China's credit tended to be channelled into investment and not consumption, new capacity required further exports to keep it utilized. By purchasing US assets with the proceeds of the exports, China funded future purchases of their own products: classic vendor financing. This monetary architecture has the effect of exaggerating divergence rather than bringing about convergence, as the gold standard had once done.

China faces many obstacles in trying to promote the renminbi as a global reserve currency to challenge the US dollar. Foremost of these is the fact that, for other parties to accept payment in renminbi, they must be confident that the currency they have been paid in will be widely accepted as means of settlement for whatever it is they need to buy. For that to happen it needs to be readily convertible into other currencies and China has consistently resisted pressure to liberalize its capital account for its own citizens. If the

Chinese themselves are not free to convert renminbi into other currencies, then there is no way of establishing a market price for the currency vis-à-vis other currencies. The exchange rate is rigged and therefore trading partners would be accepting payment in a currency the value of which is untested by the market. The Chinese have tried to maintain both domestic capital controls and promote the renminbi as an international currency by operating in effect two currency systems: offshore and onshore. A select few institutions can arbitrage between the two so that the value does not diverge too dramatically. This fudge is unlikely to be a satisfactory long-term solution. The credibility of the offshore renminbi depends on the market's confidence that the PBOC will stand behind its value, and, ironically, the credibility of the PBOC depends, or at least did depend, on its holdings of foreign exchange reserves – dollars. The offshore renminbi and indeed the renminbi itself were perhaps just a 'dollar with Chinese characteristics'!

In 2014, China's foreign exchange reserves stopped growing and began to fall. From a peak of just under four trillion dollars in mid 2014 they fell to three trillion over the next eighteen months, an alarming fall in both size and pace. This was not because China was running a trade deficit but because local Chinese were taking money offshore (in many cases illicitly), swapping their hard-earned renminbi for other currencies. Since the growth of narrow monetary aggregates in China was linked intrinsically to PBOC purchases of surplus dollars trying to come into China using renminbi, this could have had a very dramatic impact on Chinese money, credit, banking and the economy as a whole. A contraction in money supply would push interest rates up, result in non-performing loans, and potentially a very dramatic contraction in the economy. To stop this happening, the Chinese reduced cash reserve ratios so that more renminbi could be created with the backing of fewer dollars. The PBOC also intervened in the money markets adding freshly printed renminbi. In effect, they were delinking the growth in the quantity of renminbi in circulation from the speed of dollar accumulation by the central bank. Most developed countries around the world operate along these lines. The UK, Australia and the Eurozone, for example, do not accumulate foreign exchange reserves of any meaningful quantity. The acceptance or not of the pound, the Australian dollar or the euro depends on the standing of the country, its institutions and confidence that the purchasing power of the currency will be preserved. The fact that the currencies are easily convertible should one lose faith in them helps boost that confidence. For communist China though, a mercantilist exporter, this was uncharted territory.

As China changed its monetary regime from one in which renminbi were created through dollar accumulation to one in which, at least partially, the PBOC were creating renminbi independently from the balance of payments, the renminbi started to lose value. This prompted a dramatic and wide-ranging clampdown on anyone taking capital out of China. Capital controls were tightened, and the government started to reverse its more market-orientated policies. This period exposed China's monetary policy conundrums.

It is accepted that a country cannot dictate its own money supply, interest rate and the exchange rate all at the same time. If money supply rises and interest rates fall, the exchange rate may weaken. If one chooses to control the exchange rate, then interest rates and hence the money supply will have to adjust to a level in equilibrium with the chosen exchange rate. China, through the use of capital controls, was trying to circumvent this 'trilemma'. Coercion can prevent people from acting rationally, at least for a while! Furthermore, how could capital controls, which were proving necessary to support confidence in and the value of the renminbi, be compatible with promoting the renminbi as an alternative reserve currency? In the battle for the financial rewards of globalizing the renminbi, China might be risking losing the hearts and minds of its own citizenry.

It is early days in the contest to define the geographic limits of China's sphere of economic and political influence. The BRI and the internationalization of the renminbi are two linked ways in which China is expanding and deepening its reach. There are two broad options for China in this mission: liberalize the capital account and take on the West at its own game, or the path apparently chosen by Xi, which is to continue to fudge capital account convertibility but use the BRI to try and gain acceptance for the renminbi despite its limited exchangeability. Their success will depend in part on their ability to tighten controls over the nation's savings further. The recent nationalization of Anbang, a private insurance company that was investing heavily abroad, is evidence of them attempting just that. Both approaches, however, potentially jeopardize the economic gains made in recent years.

In the coming decade or so, the challenge for the West will be to contain the spread of Chinese economic and political influence in third countries where such influence is detrimental to Western interests. To do this, the West needs to demonstrate, in the face of the apparent success of the Chinese economic model, the superiority of a liberal, property-owning and democratic development model. At a minimum this will require a more principled approach from the multilateral organizations that govern the global economy and less of the duplicity that has been on display in the past two decades.

More than this, however, the Western model needs to be seen in the voting heartlands to work for a wider segment of the population than it does at present, which requires a *mea culpa* and a change of policy direction. Participation is the key to the popularity – and in a democracy that means sustainability – of any system that does not rely on coercion. Monetary policy, with its inflation bias, has strongly favoured debtors over creditors. Regulation has tended to favour large businesses over small. Trade policy has been seen to produce unjust outcomes. Crisis management has been seen to result in the socialization of losses, while profits have remained private. Risk taking must be seen to carry consequences for those who take the risks if a sense of economic and distributive justice is to return to the Western economic model. A critical look at the way the market-orientated economic model has been bastardized and contorted over the past twenty years to fit with the requirements of specific vested interests does not produce an attractive vision that third countries would necessarily wish to replicate.

China, too, faces difficult challenges in the years ahead. Its major export customers, Western consumers, are heavily indebted. Its housing stock, a key source of economic growth in the era after the global financial crisis, is looking over-built to the extent whole cities go unoccupied. Its economy has relied heavily on leverage, albeit funded domestically. Its demographic dividend is at an end and an aging population will put stresses on it social infrastructure. China's environmental degradation is problematic, its water resources exhausted. Against this background, China appears to have embarked on a more nationalistic, economic expansionism aimed at asserting her claim to be a truly global power. China's success in using economic means to spread her influence may well boil down to her ability to make the renminbi a widely accepted currency overseas, and therefore on her ability to purchase influence. That in turn perhaps depends on her ability to persuade her own citizens that they should, out of choice rather than coercion, continue to hold their wealth in 'the people's money' – an issue likely to be determined by their support, or not, for the new regime under Xi in China.

Chapter 7

Political Reform with Chinese Characteristics

Democracy substitutes election by the incompetent many for appointment by the corrupt few.
—George Bernard Shaw

RICHARD NIXON'S POLICY OF RAPPROCHEMENT with China had a clear objective: to drive a wedge between communist China and the Soviet Union. The collapse of the Soviet Union and victory in the Cold War strongly suggest the policy met its objectives. Since the end of the Cold War, however, if there has been a national as opposed to sectional interest in economic engagement with China, it has been to try and induce political change in China's communist regime, to make it more amenable to Western norms. Judging the policy by its results, it has failed. To what extent Western policymakers were convinced that they could bring about change, as opposed to the idea of providing a useful cover for corporate vested interests, is open to debate.

Since China's size meant that, should she get her economic act together, she was inevitably going to be a regional or even global power, there was certainly a feeling among some that it was better for the West to be engaged rather than confrontational, although these two extremes perhaps ignore a middle way. Nevertheless, whatever the thinking, the fact remains that the communist regime remains as antithetical to Western political norms as it ever was, despite forty years of economic reform and sixteen years and counting after WTO accession.

As if to rub salt in the wounds of those who have argued that economic engagement would lead to a more pluralistic and liberal political regime, the rise of Xi Jinping to what appears to be almost Maoist cult-like status appears to mark the start of an even more autocratic era. Accompanying his rise has been a centralization of decision-making and the abolition of term limits on the presidency. Other than a vague sense that engagement between China and the West would lead to a better understanding of each other, was there really any evidence to support the view that closer economic engagement would lead to political change? What sort of political change could realistically be expected. Does Xi Jinping's rise, often portrayed as a power grab, indicate a resurgent China or a weak China, and what does it mean for the region in terms of the potential for confrontation?

One of the problems faced by proponents of PNTR, Chinese accession to the WTO and a general policy of engagement to induce change was how to measure progress. Against what yardstick could the results of reform be measured, short of the ultimate expression of the desired reform: an end to one-party rule?

If one were to list the societal attributes that might have indicated that China was moving in the 'right direction' they might include the following: a free and critical press; the separation of the judiciary from the Party and the state; the separation of the state from the Party; and the recognition in law of some universal human rights and perhaps even local democracy.

Since very little, if any, progress was made on these issues in the years running up to or immediately after WTO accession, it is not surprising that assessments of progress did not attract the same attention that the debate on PNTR itself did. After the initial promises that the promotion of economic engagement would produce the right environment for political change, there has been a deafening silence while the policy failed to achieve its goals. There has also been a lack of critical analysis outside of specialist circles as to why the policy has failed. Only now, with the rise of President Xi and the very public changes to the constitution, has the mainstream media given this failure the attention it deserves. Even now, faced with the indisputable evidence that China has *not* moved in the direction intended, and will not do so in the foreseeable future, there is a noticeable reluctance to draw the lines of culpability or to acknowledge the very real and dramatic economic costs to the West that the failed attempt has already entailed.

It is always difficult to differentiate, with the benefit of hindsight, what has happened from what it was reasonable to expect would happen at the time decisions were made. There were several events, however, that could have exposed the naivety of Western leaders, if they really believed they could influence China's political direction.

Zhao Ziyang, perhaps, represented the best hope for a more liberal political order in China. He had been General Secretary of the CPC from 1987 to 1989, before which he had been Premier of China from 1980 to 1987. He was not only a committed economic reformer but also a genuine believer in greater participation in the political system. His support for the pro-democracy protesters in Tiananmen Square and his fervour for reform cost him his career, as he lost the support of Deng Xiaoping.

He was not alone in his beliefs nor in his fall from grace. Qiao Shi was a member of the Politburo Standing Committee for ten years and Chairman of the National People's Congress. He may have been a more cautious reformer than Zhao, but his emphasis on building *zhidu* (institutions and systems) to rein in the power of the CPC leadership and move Party rule away from the cult of the individuals occupying posts and towards a more institutional framework brought him into conflict with Jiang Zemin. His exclusion from political office after the death of Deng represented another blow to the belief that China might be moving in a more democratic direction.

Tian Jiyan was another senior liberal sidelined by the incoming leadership of Jiang. His belief that the power of competition should be brought to bear through elections for senior positions within the Party earned him the antipathy of the leadership.

These personnel changes at the top of the CPC in the late 1990s were no coincidence. They added up to the systematic purging of the liberal faction within the CPC, and were a clear demonstration that the direction the Party was heading in was diametrically opposed to that the Western policymakers and many Chinese were hoping for. They also make a nonsense of the claim that opposition to Chinese accession to the WTO would reinforce the position of hardliners and anti-democrats – these people were already well entrenched and running the CPC.

If more evidence were required that change in China was to do with economic necessity rather than an ideological commitment to reform, the persecution of the Falun Gong, which began in 1999, should surely have been sufficient. Falun Gong is a spiritual movement or cult, depending on your perspective, that began in China in 1992. By 1999 the government estimated it had about 70 million followers, making it almost as large as the CPC itself. In late 1999, the Chinese government branded the organization 'heretical' and began a clampdown. This led to the arrest, imprisonment and torture of its members. By some estimates hundreds of thousands of practitioners have been imprisoned and there have been up to 2,000 deaths as a result of the persecution.[38] Other reports put the death toll much higher and include accusations, backed with considerable evidence, that Falun Gong members have been used to provide human organs for the transplant industry on a large scale.[39]

While the degree of state sanctioning of this policy is disputed, the corruption that facilitated it exists, in large part, because of the way power works within a totalitarian system and the absence of checks and balances. While the persecution of the movement marks a dark chapter in the history of human rights abuses in China, it also should have been evidence of the CPC's unwillingness to tolerate the development of a civil society operating outside the confines of the Party.

A large part of the confusion regarding political reform in China has been one of definition. While wishful thinkers in the West may define reform as changes resulting in a move towards Western liberal norms, the Chinese authorities themselves view reforms as a never-ending process of readjusting the bureaucratic and administrative system of a totalitarian regime to increase efficiency and protect their interests. Thus there are nearly always political reforms in progress in as complex and all-encompassing a system as communist China. Sometimes, these reforms decentralize decision-making, at other times they recentralize it. There have been moves to provide checks to personal power and to institutionalize roles in the government, but recent evidence suggests that these have been easily overridden by the current leadership.

Reformers such as Zhu Rongji worked tirelessly to improve administrative efficiency and clamp down on expensive corruption that led to suboptimal economic outcomes, but that was far removed from Western notions of political reform. This confusion has allowed Western policymakers to argue that 'China is reforming' and therefore engagement is working when in fact they have been 'seeing' progress that simply did not exist if measured by the yardstick of a move towards a liberal, pluralistic society, which was after all the promise made by proponents of PNTR.

Of course, there is truth in the argument that urban home ownership, for example, and the rise of the private sector have enabled millions of Chinese to live better lives and to isolate their everyday existence to a large extent from the influence of the Party. They do so, however, under sufferance. The lack of institutional protection of property, contract and universal human rights mean the benefits of entrepreneurship and the limited liberty and protection that might bring can be abruptly and arbitrarily removed.

Xi Jinping's anti-corruption drive, which has helped remove political opposition to his rise to power, has ensnared up to 100,000 Party members, both 'flies' and 'tigers'. Among those caught up in the Party-driven purge were Zhou Yongkang, a former Politburo Standing Committee Member, and Bo Xilai, a likely contender for the role of Paramount Leader and former People's Liberation Army (PLA) top brass. At the same time, a number of high-profile businesspeople have been brought low by the purge for 'economic crimes'. The pursuit of private gain at the expense of national objectives is not, apparently, to be tolerated. One wonders how the CEOs of some Western-based multinational corporations would fare if scrutinized in such an arbitrary way! Is it any wonder that, according to one report, nearly half of Chinese millionaires are considering leaving China? Neither economic success nor political power it appears can bring security from arbitrary action.

Why has greater prosperity failed to produce irresistible pressure for political liberalization in China, as promised by supporters of economic engagement back at the turn of the century? The main reason would appear to be that the credit for this prosperity at the national level has accrued to the CPC itself. It has met its own 'key performance indicators' (KPIs) by delivering rising living standards. The Party basks in the reflective glory of the country's economic success. At the individual level, economic success has largely been achieved through connections to the CPC and in many cases by membership of the Party. The Party never lets go of the means to allocate the nation's savings and, by having near monopoly control of the allocation of capital, was able to determine the winners and losers. Add to that the omnipresent regulation and the need for bureaucratic approval for even the most basic of economic activities, and the Party, collectively and individually, has been able to purloin the lion's share of the economic benefits of growth for itself and its members. The incentive to maintain the monopoly of political power has increased proportionally with the increase in the wealth the economy generates.

Consider, for a moment, the make-up of the National People's Congress (NPC), China's parliament. According to the Huran Report,[40] the top ten richest Chinese lawmakers have an aggregate net worth of USD185 billion. In contrast, in the US, the top ten richest lawmakers have a net worth of USD1.9 billion. This hundredfold difference, in a much poorer country both in balance-sheet terms and in terms of GDP, is rather too stark to be coincidence. As Deng Xiaoping famously said, to get rich is glorious, but to do so in China without being a Party member is much harder than if you are a member. If you are one of China's 600 or so billionaires, you are most likely a member of the CPC or you are in a business partnership with one. Regardless of Party membership, recent experience suggests that you hold your wealth on sufferance of the Party hierarchy.

The inescapable conclusions to be drawn from an observation of how China's politics has evolved over the past twenty years, particularly in light of the situation that now exists, is that there has been no progress towards Western norms but neither has there been any progress towards the recognition and protection of universal human rights. Furthermore, with one man now holding the three most senior positions in the country, without time limit and apparently without effective opposition, many of the Chinese political reforms, aimed at preventing the 'cult of the personality' and promoting collective leadership and decision-making, have also failed. Arguably, the purging of the liberal faction of the CPC after the Tiananmen massacre meant that this outcome – the continuation of one-party totalitarian rule – was predictable before China's accession to the WTO.

The failure of greater prosperity to produce political change in the direction the West intended strongly suggests that Western leaders underestimated the strength of the CPC, the lack of alternative power centres but also the incentive structure that economic progress would produce. As China became richer, the incentives to hold onto power became stronger. The rewards for maintaining control of the profits of industrialization actually motivated Party members to tighten their grip on power and not to let go of the commanding heights of the economy. Technology, far from promoting freedom, just as readily could be used to suppress it. China, now the second largest economy in the world, is ruled by a strongman embarked upon a process of widening China's sphere of influence: a different type of globalization.

Chapter 8

The Legacy, the Mistakes
and a Change in Direction

To make a mistake is only an error in judgment, but to adhere
to it when it is discovered shows infirmity of character.
—Dale Turner, Author

THE ELECTION OF DONALD TRUMP to the presidency of the
United States in 2016 catapulted the West's economic relationship with China to the top of the economic and political
agenda. A more belligerent stance from the US has the potential to
disrupt the status quo but for the policy choices to have a positive
long-term impact it is important that the full ramifications of the
past relationship are properly understood. Indeed, President Trump's
election, it could be argued, is itself a reflection of some of the consequences of economic engagement with China and the beginnings
of a change to the West's policy response to it. The loss of manufacturing, the squeeze of real incomes and the growth of inequality
that have stemmed from the combination of labour market arbitrage and a domestic policy of inflation targeting were all election
issues exploited by Trump to his political advantage. More than that
though, the voting public were expressing their anger at the increasing apparent grip that business interests have on the political system.

The situation in Europe is little different. The combination of a globalized labour market, incorporating a work force of 1 billion people in China, exerting downward pressure on wages and a monetary policy aimed at preventing deflation at all costs has squeezed real wages for most people. The fact that in the Eurozone neither trade policy nor monetary policy is the responsibility of national governments adds to the sense of helplessness among the population, impotency among the national-level political class and is perhaps increasingly seen as creating a democratic deficit. It is no exaggeration to say that the West's economic relationship with China and its consequences have shaped the current political landscape on both sides of the Atlantic.

Equally, the constitutional changes in China and the concentration of power in the hands of President Xi have highlighted the complete failure of the policy of indulgent economic engagement to induce political change in China and produce a polity more sympathetic to liberal values – quite the contrary. China's unique brand of mercantilist economic nationalism, pursued with the acquiescence of the West, has produced a big enough economy to give China meaningful global clout. The speed and scale of China's economic transformation since WTO accession, far from producing a political system more in keeping with Western norms has cemented the CPC in power. Economic success has also increased the financial rewards for political control over the economy and therefore the incentive to retain power.

The Party's political monopoly remains intact but so too does its effective control over the legal system and the economic resources of the country. Party and state remain almost indistinguishable from one another. China's rise to dominance in global manufacturing has brought her influence in countries that provide both the resources that are her inputs and the markets for her output. Chinese companies engaged in this trade and investment enjoy the total support of and are often controlled by the state and therefore the

Party. The inevitable result of a state-sanctioned, export-orientated, manufacturing economy is a spread of Chinese influence across a sphere defined by the limits and degree of her economic engagement. Third countries too, neighbours, suppliers and competitors, are seeing the political and economic ramifications of their trade and investment links to China.

If a policy of indulgent engagement with China has failed from a Western point of view in its stated political aims, it has also produced a very unbalanced and in many ways debilitating economic relationship. Understanding how and why is a prerequisite to designing policies to put economic relations on a more even footing. As is now well understood, trade imbalances between China and the West grew exponentially following China's WTO accession. Equally importantly, but perhaps less well understood, the FDI that poured into China from multinational companies, when combined with the knock-on effects of this investment, was the major driver of Chinese productivity improvement and hence economic growth. China has a strong national interest in the continuation of these investment flows and in keeping unhindered access to overseas markets. Whether Chinese policymakers fully appreciate the impact that foreign investment has had on their economy is debatable.

From a Western perspective the flip side of China's export success was the substitution of Chinese imports for domestic-made manufacturing goods with accompanying loss of employment and income. The shed workers have not been redeployed more productively elsewhere as theory would suggest, as demonstrated by the decline in overall productivity growth in the West. FDI to China came at the expense of productivity-enhancing investment at home. And the labour arbitrage has put downward pressure on household incomes. From a societal point of view, economic engagement with China has been a disaster. Of course, cheaper manufactured imports are a good thing for the consumer, but this benefit has been netted away by a policy of inflation targeting that pushed up the cost of non-tradable services and asset prices – what good is a cheap washing machine if one cannot afford a home to put it in? One may well ask: What were Western policymakers thinking encouraging and facilitating a deflationary policy of globalization if existing levels of indebtedness meant that deflation could not be tolerated? Furthermore, the easy monetary policy aimed at trying to avoid deflation encouraged more debt accumulation that, should the policy fail, would make the fallout even worse. The fact that Western central banks have quintupled the size of their balance sheets since China's accession to the WTO and yet have struggled to produce levels of inflation consistent with their targets shows just how great the deflationary pressure from China has been. Such a balance sheet expansion would have been universally thought to produce hyper-inflation prior to 2001. The combination of trade with China and inflation targeting could only lead to falling real living standards for most people in the West.

Of course, not everyone in the West has been a loser from this process. While the national interest may well have been badly served by engagement with China, some sections of society have done well. The sharp rise in corporate profitability, as a result multinationals being able to exploit the cheap labour available in China and 'off-shore' their production, was a boon to the owners of capital and represented an income transfer away from workers who sell labour to the shareholders and of course the top managers who were incentivized through share options or whose pay was linked to corporate performance. Over the eighteen years or so since China's accession to the WTO, this income transfer from households to companies approximates to a cumulative USD12 trillion or so. The lobbying efforts of the mid and late 1990s have paid off handsomely as far as multinationals are concerned. The shortfall in household income has been made up by increased consumer borrowing for homes and living expenses in an unsustainable effort to prevent a decline in living standards. The windfall for companies, however, has not produced a corresponding de-leveraging in the corporate sector. Rising profitability coupled with remuneration incentive structures based on share price performance and measures of capital efficiency encouraged share buy-backs and higher leverage. The result of this income transfer and its impact on income distribution within Western society has been well documented; it has added to the growth of populism and helped discredit the current capitalist system in the eyes of many.

Multinationals have not had it all their own way. While the use of China as a low-cost manufacturing base from which to export back to home countries has been an unmitigated success, access to the Chinese domestic market has been more limited than was hoped and the dreamed-of profits to be made there have proved largely illusory. Even now after eighteen years of trying, the size of American corporate profits made by selling products made in China to the Chinese amount to no more than 2% of total corporate profits: almost a rounding error.[41]

The counterpart to the trade and investment relationship with China has been ever more desperate efforts to prevent the deflationary impact of globalization from producing an overall fall in prices in the West. The rise in financial and real asset prices, which has been the consequence of unprecedently easy monetary policy (negative real interest rates and money printing), has distributed income and wealth away from productive parts of the Western economy and towards those involved in financial markets and real estate markets. A disproportionate amount of the good things in life are being enjoyed by those involved in asset jobbing and financial management. As importantly, by driving the price of homes and an old-age pension up, a generational divide has appeared that poses a severe political risk. While the owners of assets over the past few decades have seen nominal prices rise, those who were too young to own assets now face the prospect of having to buy them at inflated prices or not buy them at all. Any system of political economy depends on participation. An ever-increasing proportion of the voting and working-age population of Western democracies are not able to participate in the ownership of either capital or homes.

The legacy in the West of economic engagement with China is a more heavily indebted society than at any point in its modern history. It is a society in which inequality has grown, productivity growth has disappointed and participation in property ownership is falling. As democratically elected politicians struggle to fulfil their side of the perceived social contract, populism is on the rise. In the democracies of the West, the unequal but more importantly unjust outcomes of engagement with China have produced not just a change in political opinion but a loss of confidence in the system itself.

Gone are the apparent certainties that existed at the time of the collapse of the Soviet Union. The confidence that, given time, liberal democracy would be adopted around the world because it was the natural choice for free people to make, and that freedom could not be deferred indefinitely, was misplaced. The hubris of that era has been replaced by a sense that power rests with an elite that does not serve the population at large but rather narrow vested interests, and the accession of China to the WTO serves as a good example of that. The ad hoc and unprincipled handling of the last global financial crisis, together with the institutional failings that were laid bare by it, has done more to foster this belief and to discredit capitalism in the eyes of the electorate than any event since the Great Depression. Yet national politicians too, particularly in Europe, feel far from omnipotent. The delegation upwards of political power to multilateral and supranational organizations, and sideways to central banks, means that the ability to rectify policy mistakes has to a large extent been taken out of their hands. An Italian prime minister or a French president, for example, has no control over monetary policy and no control over trade policy, so if those two factors have been major drivers of the economic situation Italy and France now find themselves in, is it any wonder that there is disillusionment with the political system? Furthermore, is it a surprise that an emasculated national-level political class resorts to feathering their own nests and political expediency? Responsibility without power is perhaps as dangerous as power without responsibility.

The best protection for property rights in a democratic system is surely widespread ownership. As the economic horrors of the 1970s fade in the collective memory of the electorate, it becomes even more important for the preservation of the market-orientated system that participation levels increase, and not decrease. Yet home ownership is falling in many parts of the free world and as income-constrained consumers fail to save, direct involvement in capital markets is on the decline among the young too. An ever-widening constituency has a vested interest in asset price deflation and is disinterested in the protection of private property rights.

The situation in China is, of course, very different. In raw economic terms China as a nation has boomed with an economy now nine times larger than at the time of accession to the WTO. Politically though, her institutions have failed to develop alongside the economy as had been hoped. Inequalities of wealth and income rival and by some measures exceed those in the West.

From the perspective of the Communist Party of China, economic engagement with the rest of the world has been an unmitigated success, bringing undreamt-of wealth to China's communist elite. The technological capabilities of the country have been transformed in a short period of time. Living standards have risen and the new prosperity has reflected well on the Party, its leaders and their policies. Hundreds of millions of Chinese have been lifted out of poverty and the average Chinese person enjoys an income not too far below the global average. The benefits have been far from evenly spread, however. Life expectancy has risen from 72 years to

76 years since the turn of the century. Using the IMF definition of the poverty line (an income of USD1.90 per day at Purchasing Power Parity for 2011 dollars), the number of Chinese living below the poverty line has fallen from 750 million in 1990 to 500 million in 2000 to about 30 million now. It is an extraordinary achievement in one sense, but is there any reason in an economy of eleven trillion dollars, and eight thousand dollars per head, why anyone should live on less than seven hundred dollars per year? As of 2013, nearly half a billion Chinese were living on less than USD5.50 per day or two thousand dollars a year. The lion's share of the benefits of the export-driven growth boom have accrued to the well-connected and to Party members.

Physically, in terms of housing stock and infrastructure, the country has been modernized and, in many instances, finds itself with more superior infrastructure assets than the so-called developed world. All this has been achieved without the Party having to cede control of the commanding heights of the economy nor its monopoly on political power. The Party, through the state-owned financial institutions, still controls and allocates the majority of capital. SOEs still dominate the strategically important industries and, while private entrepreneurship thrives in some segments of the economy, it does so under the watchful eye of the Party, which retains the ability to sequestrate the benefits of wealth creation as and when it chooses. Economic criminality in China is very much in the eye of the beholder.

China has now moved on to the next phase of her 'National Rejuvenation'. The achievement of some of her stated goals is very much in everyone's interests. Improving the quality of her growth will be beneficial to the environment, for example. Others may bring China into conflict with the democratic world. China's rise to dominate global manufacturing has increased her influence over countries that supply her with raw materials, while the West's retreat has eroded its influence. China's apparent economic success is thought by some to demonstrate an alternative route to development, and one that appeals to the kleptocratic or dictatorial tendencies of some leaders in the developing world. The West has helped create a global rival and the cost of competition is unlikely to be low.

From a Western point of view, the policy of economic engagement with China has failed. If the intention was to mould China into its own image, the policy has been counterproductive. By enabling a rapid rise in living standards in China, trade and investment have helped validate the Party's polices and legitimize the regime. For now, the CPC seem as well entrenched as it ever has been and policy towards China should be based on the twin assumptions: (a) that this is likely to be the case for a considerable period to come and (b) that there is little the West can do about it. The West underestimated the resilience of one-party rule and the incentives to hold on to power that increased affluence would bring. A capital-owning class, whose existence depended on the arbitrary exercise of political power, did not turn against the power that was the source of its livelihood: it did not bite the hand that fed it. It is perhaps only when the economic system starts to fail to deliver prosperity that that may happen.

China's economy is far from bullet proof, however, and the leadership is aware of the threats that over-indebtedness and demographics might pose to the standard of living and hence to Party legitimacy. The risk of over-indebtedness is a legacy of the current economic architecture in both the West and in China. Furthermore, the escalation of trade friction into the potential for trade war has highlighted the vulnerability of China's model. With that in mind, the criterion for judging success, and therefore legitimacy, is being redefined, in part towards a more nationalistic interpretation of 'rejuvenation': the Belt and Road Initiative forms a part of that policy. At one level, this represents a preemptive move to try and minimize the impact from a more belligerent attitude from the West.

The lop-sided and destructive legacy of economic engagement between the West and China this century raises the question: What could have been done differently to produce a more balanced result? The mistakes that Western leaders made, both in the run-up to China's accession to the WTO and in dealing with its aftermath, were manifold. Allowing an economy of China's potential scale, with a workforce of its size and at the price that prevailed at the time, into the global trade system was always going to be problematic. To allow this to happen without first insisting on capital account convertibility and a floating exchange rate, which would have allowed for the required adjustments to take place, was negligent in the extreme. Without a clear and enforceable road-map for the withdrawal of state involvement from the commanding heights of the economy, particularly the financial system, the mercantilist model was left intact. In practice, the de-politicization of the banking system would have been hard to achieve and almost impossible to enforce and monitor. These though were the minimum requirements for ensuring a more even relationship than the one that has evolved. Too much faith was placed in the ability of the WTO to force a convergence of legal standards and compliance with the obligations of membership – a function of the gargantuan nature of the task rather than a reflection of the competence of the WTO. Too much faith was placed in the willingness of China to play by the rule book and not enough was done to enforce compliance.

These mistakes, perhaps born of hubris and naivety, were compounded by those conceived in panic. Fighting the deflationary impact of one policy mistake by trying to engender inflation through credit expansion has compounded the error to the extent that any change in direction now runs the risk of being extremely painful to the point of jeopardizing the West's political and economic system. Underlying these mistakes, however, was a close, and at times pernicious, relationship between big business, high finance and the political class in the West. The legislative process was purloined by those whose interests lay in the continuation of an economic architecture that was serving their institutions and interests well but their countries badly.

The failure to recognize for what it was the deflationary, supply-induced shock to Western economies following China's accession to the WTO led directly to the housing bubble and the global financial crisis. The continuation of easy monetary policy after the global financial crisis has led to yet more debt being accumulated and the postponement of the reckoning that is required. The policy has made a change of direction both riskier and potentially more painful. But is it too late?

Policies aimed at protecting financial institutions from the consequences of their own mistakes have made the global financial system as a whole very vulnerable. Similarly, inaction in the face of China's mercantilism, to protect the multinationals that have invested heavily in China and who have benefited so dramatically from globalization, has only served to elongate and deepen an unfair and imbalanced economic relationship that has been debilitating to society as a whole and raise the stakes involved in a move to reverse the process.

The starting point for redressing the imbalances of the current economic architecture must surely be that it is not in the West's interest to become dependent on communist China. Yet it is almost impossible to buy a personal computer or a smartphone that is not, at least partly, made in China. The 'Made in China 2025' policy, designed to bring China's mercantilist approach to cutting-edge industries such as artificial intelligence and robotics suggests that there is no recognition on China's part of the need for a change in approach. On the contrary, from the Chinese perspective, it is an approach that has worked well and 'Made in China 2025' now poses a real threat to Western technological leadership. A lurch towards autarky or at least the threat of one, as a precursor to a fairer more balanced global trading system, should not necessarily be condemned by liberal advocates of free trade. A degree of disengagement may well bring home to policymakers in Beijing the degree to which China has in the past and continues to benefit from unfettered access to foreign investment and trade, often at the expense of the West.

If an economic policy of indulging China has failed in its stated aims, would a policy of disengagement work and at what cost? Is that the only alternative, or indeed even an alternative, to a continuation of the current policy that is so debilitating for liberal democracy? The early indications from the first, perhaps clumsy, moves to bring China seriously to the negotiating table are encouraging. The Trump administration has taken on the task of confronting China's unfair trade and investment practices with a robustness that is perhaps long overdue. The ineffectual protests of past administrations have cost valuable time during which China has become more powerful and Western institutions more vulnerable.

A highly indebted West cannot countenance higher interest rates without potentially destroying the financial system. So, if disengagement from China were to involve a rise in inflation, due to a supply-side shock, the West would have to live with higher inflation for a while until that temporary shock was absorbed or accept a probably vicious recession with accompanying debt defaults that would require a repeat bail-out of the financial system.

The risk from the supply-side shock is that long-term inflationary expectations were raised and that, what would have been a temporary period of higher inflation, became elongated, requiring central bank action. Fortunately, China does not have a monopoly over cheap labour, and other countries, those that have lost out to China, would fill the void, to some extent at least. A rebalancing of manufacturing away from China towards eastern Europe, Latin America, India, Mexico and Africa would perhaps help nurture those economies. Technology may also come to the aid of the West in this regard through robotics and automation. Over the longer term, the West can live well without trade with China although such an outcome may not be optimal in the short term. It is more doubtful whether the CPC could live without trade with the West without fundamental change in its economic structure. In the shorter term though, the disruption to global supply chains, into which China is heavily integrated, would potentially be enormous but there is no easy way out of the conundrum the West has put itself in.

The same vested interests that argued for PNTR and engagement with China will, no doubt, resist a more belligerent stance. Corporate profitability would suffer but income would potentially be redistributed towards households through tightness in the labour market. A more proactive pushing back on China's economic mercantilism, requiring results rather than promises, would potentially put the CPC in a difficult position. Their own constituents' tolerance for economic pain is limited given their own indebtedness, their legitimacy rests on rising living standards. Whether or not a policy of economic belligerence induces change or not, the cost of continuing on the current path, both monetary and political, risks being far higher.

The main argument against the imposition of tariffs or quotas on trade with China is that they will be self-defeating: they will lead to a loss of economic welfare in the West. Higher import prices will erode real incomes by pushing up the import component of inflation. Where the higher prices are for finished goods (such as white goods), the higher costs of those imports will leave less money for households to spend on other things. Where the goods are inputs to the manufacturing process, such as steel, they will damage the profitability of the users of those materials or lead to high prices for the goods that they go into, such as cars. Yet as we have seen during the reverse process, during the period of engagement, the outcomes are more dynamic and less predictable than that.

While there is economic rationale in the arguments against tariffs and quotas, any loss in economic well-being must be weighed against the costs a dominant China would be able to impose on the West and the benefits of restoring a sense of economic justice to the Western system that engagement with China has destroyed. Furthermore, there is no more certainty in the arguments against tariffs and quotas than there was in the economic arguments in favour of PNTR. If China has indeed won market share for reasons other than comparative advantage, a reversal of that situation could lead to a more efficient allocation of resources. Could it not be the case, for example, that higher nominal wages in the West may result from effectively reducing the supply of cheap Chinese labour? Tariffs would effectively increase the cost of Chinese labour, whereas quotas effectively reduce the supply. Could higher wages not compensate for the impact of higher imported inflation? Would not the Federal Reserve and other central banks have to 'run less hard' to meet their inflation targets as a result of higher imported inflation? Would not a rebalancing of inflation away from nontradable goods and towards tradable goods unwind some of the negative distributive impacts of the existing polices?

In a competitive economy it is returns on capital (profits) that might bear the brunt of higher input costs rather than end prices and this could help redistribute GDP from companies to households in a way that is desperately needed. Of course, there would be losers and winners. Falling asset prices (homes, bonds and equities) may well result from a rise in the level of interest rates required to meet inflation targets and corporate profits may fall as a percentage of GDP. The question to be answered though is: Is this a price worth paying for a more inclusive and sustainable capitalist system or would we rather risk a rejection of the entire system at the ballot box with the loss of prosperity and freedom that that would inevitably bring? The experience of the period 2001–18 is that real spending power for Western households has stagnated during the period of engagement with China. Can we be so sure that the same interest groups that failed to predict such an outcome are correct when predicting the same outcome from the opposite policy? There is unlikely to be a cost-free remedy to the current economic malaise even if China cooperates. The issue is one of which segments of which society meet the cost.

It need not be the case that a more aggressive policy towards trade with China involves a prolonged period of tariffs and quotas. If, as is strongly implied by the analysis in this book, it is in China's interests to keep an open trading and investment relationship with the West, they should be receptive to the idea of a more balanced outcome from economic engagement. This would involve encouraging consumer spending and redistributing income to households in order to assist the adjustment. What has been missing from Western policy has been both a united front and a willingness to countenance disengagement and therefore put pressure on the Chinese to cooperate. The growing realization that the period of engagement has had a debilitating impact on our democracy and economy should help remove the taboo around a frank and all-encompassing analysis of both the benefits and flaws in the free trade argument. The theory of free trade is compelling, the actual practice less so. 'Mutual benefit' needs to be the guiding principle of economic interaction with China. Whether, under the current leadership, the US, the EU and their other allies are of a mind to put up a united front to China on trade and related issues remains to be seen, but to repeat the mistakes of the accession process by allowing themselves to played off against each other would be inexcusable when the stakes are so high.

If, as seems increasing likely, the economic relationship between the West and China is undergoing a paradigm shift, many of the institutional arrangements that have prevailed during the period of 'indulgent engagement' may well change too. The dollar standard is unlikely to survive in a global environment where the second largest economy and largest trading nation in the world de-links its own money supply from dollar accumulation. What role will there be for the WTO if the largest bilateral trading relationship in the world (that between China and the US) operates in a system outside of its rule book, as it is starting to do? The breakdown in the current economic relationship between China and the West may well produce calls for more global governance, when the evidence suggests that democracies in the West appear to be calling for less centralization and more localization with the increase in accountability that goes with it.

The biggest legacy, however, from the last two decades of the West's trading relationship with China is unprecedented indebtedness, inequality and extraordinarily elevated property and financial asset prices relative to incomes which jeopardize the stability of the global financial system. As Herbert Stein said, 'If something cannot go on forever it will stop.' True as this may be, in the case of the West's economic relationship with China, the inaction of policymakers can be put down to expediency. The continuation of the current situation is simply not an option. Western leaders owe it to their constituents to put aside vested interests and proactively develop a policy that will redress the imbalances caused by the last eighteen years of indulgent economic engagement with China. This may well have to involve demonstrating to the Chinese a willingness to disengage. It will also require a consistent, united front from Western nations. When faced with a concerted and robust policy response from its trading partners, only then will China and the CPC recognize that their own interests rest in making the changes necessary to ensure a sustainable global trade and investment regime.

ENDNOTES

1. See, for example, John Giles: What is China's true unemployment rate? October 2004.
2. Bill Clinton: Speech on the China Trade Bill, Johns Hopkins University, March 2000.
3. Ibid.
4. Mike Jendrzejcky: Testimony before the Ways and Means Committee, February 2000.
5. Madeleine Albright: https://1997-2001.state.gov/statements/2000/000406.html
6. Doug Bandow: https://www.cato.org/publications/commentary/trade-china-business-profits-or-human-rights 2000.
7. Ibid.
8. Ibid.
9. Bill Clinton: Speech on the China Trade Bill, Johns Hopkins University, March 2000.
10. David E. Sanger: US blames allies for undercutting its China policy. *New York Times*, 12 June 1996.
11. Ibid.
12. For an excellent summary of the activities of the New China Lobby and the lobbying campaign for unconditional economic engagement with China, see Richard Bernstein and Ross Munro: *The Coming Conflict with China*. Vintage, 1998.

13. William H. Overholt: *China: The Next Economic Superpower.* Weidenfeld & Nicolson, 1993.

14. World Bank: China 2020: China Engaged, 1997. The report provides a comprehensive overview of China's economic development together with some predictions about the prospects of the economy from 1997.

15. Michael J. Enright: *Developing China: The Remarkable Impact of Foreign Direct Investment.* New York, Routledge, 2017.

16. President Clinton: Speech on the China Trade Bill, Johns Hopkins University, March 2000.

17. Bill Clinton: Speech on the China Trade Bill, Johns Hopkins University, March 2000.

18. A copy of the 13th Plan can be found at http://en.ndrc.gov.cn/newsrelease/201612/P020161207645765233498.pdf

19. Supachai Panitchpakdi and Mark L. Clifford: *China and the WTO: Changing China, Changing World Trade.* John Wiley & Sons, 2002.

20. For a full explanation of the degree to which China has flouted the terms and spirit of its accession agreement, see '2017 Report to Congress on China's WTO compliance' (https://ustr.gov/sites/default/files/files/Press/Reports/China%202017%20WTO%20Report.pdf).

21. A copy of the report is available at https://enforcement.trade.gov/download/prc-nme-status/prc-nme-review-final-103017.pdf

22. It is undoubtedly true that China's currency does not enjoy free convertibility on the capital account, and that a closed capital account has offered policymakers degrees of freedom that are unavailable to countries that do allow free currency convertibility.

23. The article available at http://www.scmp.com/news/china/economy/article/2027407/communist-party-top-boss-chinas-state

-firms-xi-jinping-asserts from the SCMP reports President Xi's determination to keep the CPC in control of SOEs.

24. Reported in the China daily: http://www.chinadaily.com.cn/china/2015twosession/2015-03/11/content_19776066.htm
25. Quoted in the *Financial Times*: https://www.ft.com/content/3c521faa-baa6-11e5-a7cc-280dfe875e28
26. https://en.wikipedia.org/wiki/Guanxi
27. https://www.forbes.com/sites/russellflannery/2017/11/15/chinas-richest-2017-real-estate-developer-hui-ka-yan-takes-top-spot-for-1st-time/#6697f7f451bc (November 2017).
28. All numbers from company annual reports.
29. Bureau of Labour Statistics (BLS) data.
30. NBS data.
31. Hu Angang: Is China the root cause of deflations?
32. Steven B. Kamin, Mario Marazzi and John W. Schindler: Is China 'exporting deflation'? FRB paper 791, January 2004.
33. BLS data.
34. Alan Greenspan: *The Age of Turbulence*. Penguin, 2007.
35. Ben Bernanke: Speech to the National Economist Club, November 2002. The text can be found at https://www.federalreserve.gov/boarddocs/speeches/2002/20021121/
36. Joshua Ramo: *The Beijing Consensus*. Foreign Policy Centre, 2004.
37. An excellent overview of the Latin American debt crisis by Sims and Romero can be found at https://www.federalreservehistory.org/essays/latin_american_debt_crisis
38. China: the crackdown on Falun Gong and other so-called 'heretical organizations'. Amnesty International, 23 March 2000.
39. David Kilgour and David Matas (6 July 2006, revised 31 January 2007): An independent investigation into allegations of organ harvesting of Falun Gong practitioners in China.

40. See the Hurun Report available at http://www.hurun.net/EN/ Home/
41. According to the BEA, total US net corporate profits now amount to USD1.9 trillion. Applying a 10% net margin to USD250 billion of sales in China of goods made in China would give a profit of USD25 billion.

INDEX